Praise for Sant Rajinder Singh's books

"Sant Rajinder Singh Ji explains how peace can be created through meditation and inner reflection. There will be no lasting peace unless individual human beings have some sense of inner peace. To create inner peace it is necessary to calm the mind, hence the importance of meditation. I greatly appreciate Sant Rajinder Singh Ji's contribution here to the goal of peace that we are all working towards."
    —H.H. the Dalai Lama

"Rajinder Singh's deep wisdom and realizations emerge from divine love and inner fulfillment."
    —Deepak Chopra

"…deep, clearly written book about practical spirituality that helps us let go of the self-made blocks that interfere with the awareness that we are one with God and each other.…"
    —Gerald G. Jampolsky, M.D., author of *Love Is Letting Go of Fear*

"Firmly rooted in traditional wisdom, the author faces contemporary questions and challenges squarely and in a nonsectarian way.… to bring the seed of peace within us to fruition in daily life and the world we live in."
    —Brother David Steindl-Rast

"…an inspiring and informative source that speaks to both beginners and experienced travelers on the path of life."
    —educator, recording artist, and musician Steven Halpern

"Meditation empowers us in two spiritual arenas. First, it leads us to inner peace and fulfillment.... Second, meditation allows us to use our talents and skills to make the world a better place to live. Rajinder Singh elaborates on these ideas beautifully. He says that by mastering meditation, we not only attain personal fulfillment, we become an instrument for bringing peace and joy to those around us."
— Mary Nurrie Stearns, Editor, *Personal Transformation*

"Rajinder Singh expounds his theory that true peace and happiness can only come from within: the skill lies in learning how to tap into them."
— *Here's Health* magazine

Spiritual Pearls for Enlightened Living

Also by Rajinder Singh

RAJINDER SINGH

Spiritual Pearls

for Enlightened Living

*An inspirational collection of stories and anecdotes
from the world's wisdom traditions that provide
guidance for enlightened living.*

Radiance Publishers

© Copyright 2006 Radiance Publishers
Naperville, Illinois, U.S.A.

Library of Congress Control Number: 2006930577

ISBN-10 0-918224-52-7
ISBN-13 978-0-918224-52-1

Illustrations by Valerie Poole
Book design by Valerie Brewster, Scribe Typography
Printed in Canada by Printcrafters, Winnipeg

This book is dedicated to my spiritual Masters,
Sant Kirpal Singh Ji Maharaj and
Sant Darshan Singh Ji Maharaj, for the
spiritual Light they brought to the world.

Contents

Introduction

In this fast-paced age of technological advances, life was supposed to be easier, yet many find the daily stresses overwhelming. People have little free time to relax or find solutions to their problems. With compassionate understanding of the plight of modern readers, Sant Rajinder Singh Ji Maharaj offers us this precious book. The easy-to-read gems in *Spiritual Pearls for Enlightened Living* provide fresh insights to cope with the complexities of our times and help to deepen our spiritual perspectives.

As a teacher of Peace Studies at the university level, I find it refreshing to see this book which offers readers an opportunity to draw upon the collective wisdom of peoples' experiences, past and present, from around the world. One of the courses I most enjoy teaching is called "Wisdom Traditions of the World's Religions and Cultures." In it we explore the rich diversity of human experience, seeking to identify the common threads needed to build human unity. Sant Rajinder Singh's pearls will be a welcomed addition to the literature in our course. I would submit that this kind of learning that the book exemplifies should ideally be available not only for college students but for people of all ages enrolled in what might be called the ongoing "university of the universe." Sant Rajinder Singh draws upon his broad knowledge and respect for the teachings of enlightened beings from many religions and cultures to bring home timeless spiritual truths.

I especially appreciate the way the author has included teaching stories about philosophers, teachers, saints, kings, and commoners from different cultures and times, to convey uplifting truths to put us in touch with the reservoir of spiritual resources within each of us. Included are anecdotes about the Buddha, Leonardo da Vinci, Maulana Rumi, Thomas Edison, Ernest Shackleton, Mother Teresa, and many others. Like a delicious sweet, each story can be savored and reflected upon for some time afterward. We learn how human folly and suffering can be transformed by learning humility and forgiveness. In fifty-two teaching stories ranging from overcoming adversity to attaining enlightenment, the tales and their underlying life lessons tap into a broad canvas of human experience and illustrate how to:

- face adversity with calm and stability
- overcome anger to maintain our peace of mind
- find lasting happiness
- learn contentment, acceptance, and "letting go"
- achieve success toward our goals, both mundane and spiritual
- conquer fear of death
- experience inner spiritual realms of beauty and bliss beyond this physical one.

As a musician produces music and as a poet writes verses, Sant Rajinder Singh tells each anecdote to uplift us into seeing life from a higher angle of vision. He encourages us to tap into our higher self and think, speak, and act from a place of wisdom. His optimism that we can find peace and love in a troubled world is "contagious."

Each story that he offers contains a pearl of wisdom to be taken to heart and put into practice and can enlighten us and bring joy into our lives. Spending time in the company of this book gives us an opportunity to read the words of saints and mystics who came throughout history to serve humankind.

This collection was selected from talks by Sant Rajinder Singh given over many years at several major meditation centers in India and in the

United States. Beautifully illustrated by Valerie Poole, these illuminating stories with their underlying messages are presented with a balance of wisdom, humor, love, and everyday common sense. They have been inspiring millions of people over the past seventeen years to develop their higher self through meditation and positive human values.

Through a life devoted to meditation on the spiritual Light within and achieving spiritual realization, Sant Rajinder Singh points out ways for us to experience spirituality. Using references from diverse wisdom traditions, he threads together a path of an enlightened life. *Spiritual Pearls for Enlightened Living* could well become a classic, as Sant Rajinder Singh unveils the mystery of how people everywhere can have firsthand experience of the divine and attain lasting happiness.

Dr. Art Stein,
Professor of Political Science/Honors and Co-Convener of Center for Nonviolence and Peace Studies, University of Rhode Island

𝄪

Spiritual Pearls for Enlightened Living

Facing Adversity

Dealing with Adversity and Happiness

All human beings face the ups and downs of life. They are part of the human existence and cannot be avoided. The question is, are we going to lose our peace of mind and become unstable as we face these highs and lows on the roadway of life? If we let ourselves become affected by everything that comes our way in life, we will feel as if we are on a perpetual roller coaster. We will move from the heights of ecstasy to the depths of despair and back to ecstasy again from one moment to the next. These constant variations often lead to a sense of fear, anxiety, and panic because we never know what will happen next. Over time, this state of fear and anxiety becomes a part of our nature and we are not able to relax.

Since we do not seem to have much control over the ups and downs of life, how can we learn to live a life of peace and relaxation? The following story gives us some clue:

A king called together all his wise counselors and advisors. He posed to them a question: "O advisors, I wish that my inner self were filled with stability. I find that I am always subject to the ups and downs of life and they throw me off balance. Can you find something that will help me feel joyful when in a state of unhappiness, and something that will remind me of sadness when I am in a state of happiness? Find me something that I can keep with me to help me stay in a calm, stable mood despite whatever is happening around me."

The advisors put their heads together and thought long and hard about what the king requested. Finally, they came up with a solution. They went back to the king.

The king saw them approaching with a small box.

"We found a solution for you, O King," the advisors said. "Open the box."

When the king opened it, he found within a small ring.

"Look at the inscription," they told him.

The inscription in the ring said, "This too shall pass."

These four simple words helped the king and can help us maintain a sense of balance when we face the highs and lows of life. When we become too ecstatic and happy, we need to remember that things will not always be that way, and we should not be disappointed or depressed when the happy times pass. When we become too depressed or unhappy, these four words can serve as a reminder to us that the pain is only temporary, and happy days will come again.

We can stay at an even keel through the storms and sunny days of life by finding a calm center. We can reach this still point through meditation and prayer. Within us are all the riches of divinity. We are not just the body and the mind, but the soul. The soul is filled with Light, love, and joy. Why? It is connected all the time with the source of divinity, the creative Power, which is also all Light, love, and joy. The creative Power and the soul are made of the same essence. If we spend some time daily within the silence of our soul, we will be connected with a place of bliss. Then the outer circumstances of our life will not affect us. We will not be troubled by the temporary phases of life. We can learn to find a still center, filled with peace and balance, which will provide us with permanent happiness despite the outer variations of life.

Next time we face pain, remember that "This too shall pass." Those four words may help us pass through the discomfort with more confidence and faith. It will remind us to find our still center of peace through meditation.

Next time we are in state of great joy, remember that "This too shall pass," so we can enjoy the moments and not grow depressed when they end. It will remind us that even if this joy ends and a hardship comes, other times of joy will one day return. It will remind us to find our still center of peace through meditation, for that provides lasting happiness.

Facing the Challenges of Life

There is a story of a young man who went to college. He was different from the other college students in one respect. The boy had to get around college in a wheelchair. Despite his handicap he was well liked. He was a friendly person with an optimistic attitude.

The boy worked hard and won many academic honors. His classmates had great respect for him. One day a schoolmate asked him, "What has caused your physical handicap?"

The college student said, "I developed cerebral palsy as a baby."

The friend asked him, "What is your secret? How can you live with such great misfortune yet still face the world with a smile and confidence?"

The college student replied with a smile, "You see, the disease never touched my heart and soul."

How many times do we find ourselves or our family members complaining about minor discomforts? Throughout life we face some physical challenges. As children we can have childhood diseases. Throughout the year, we can have many ailments. When we overeat we may get a stomachache. Many of us complain and whine over all these.

Yet if we look around us we find many people with severe handicaps. We find people who have lost a limb, or who have a terminal illness. Among these we find people who learn to live life to its fullest even with these challenges. Like the college student in the story, they do not let the problems of their physical body affect their heart or their soul.

We are soul. Our true self is spirit. The body is but a covering over the soul. Spirituality is a process of discovering our true self within.

Meditation and prayer help us to separate our soul from the body so we can discover who we really are.

Many of us own cars. At times the car breaks down and goes into an auto repair shop. While we may be inconvenienced for a while by having to rent a car or by needing a family member or friend to drive us around, we do not feel as though our life is over. We realize the car is but a vehicle by which our physical body can get around. Similarly, the body is but a vehicle for our soul. At times it may break down. But it does not need to affect our soul. We can learn to keep our spirits high. We can make the best of life, whether we have a broken vehicle or not.

At some point in our lives, our body will show signs of aging. Although the Genome Project is trying to uncover the gene responsible for aging, and a day may come when more people live well beyond a hundred years, there will come a time when our body does not function as well as it did when we were younger. But we should not let that deter us. There are many people who suffer ill health in their aging years, but do not let that stop them from finding peace in their soul.

Similarly, we can make the best use of our life no matter what our physical challenges. By spending time in communion with God and drinking of God's love, we can spread love to all we meet. We can do that no matter what our physical circumstance. If we are at home due to a sickness, we can still bring love into the lives of the family members who are caring for us. After all, it is but our physical vesture that is ill; our soul is always in the best of health.

If we live like the college student in the story, we will not let our physical challenges affect our heart and soul. An optimistic, positive attitude will help us overcome the challenges and we can bring joy into our life and the lives of others.

Overcoming Anger

Replacing Anger with Love

Once, Mother Teresa was asked by someone, "Do you ever become angered by all the examples of social injustice that you see around you in India and in other parts of the world in which you work?" Mother Teresa beautifully answered, "Why should I expend energy in anger when I can expend it in love?"

This response by Mother Teresa illustrates a high angle of vision by which we can also lead our lives. Every day, we find many situations that can provoke anger. Sometimes we become angry when someone hurts or offends us. There are instances in which we become angry when we see others being hurt. We may find cases of social injustice in which a group of people in society is being treated unfairly. In each of these cases, we may feel that a wrong has been committed. We may not be able to ignore what is happening. The difference is in how we respond to injustice. We have the capability to make choices. We can either react out of anger, or we can overcome and replace the anger with love. Mother Teresa chose to overcome anger with love.

There is plenty of anger and violence in the world. In every town and village, in every home, one finds explosions of anger. To respond to this anger with more anger only fuels the flames. We do not put out fire by fanning the flames. We have to smother the fire. Similarly, we do not put out fires of anger by adding more fire to them. We can smother the fire of anger with love.

Rather than add one more angry voice to a dispute, we should add the balm of sweetness to cool down the tempers of others. Rather than add to the vibrations of the atmosphere with an angry thought, we should send loving thoughts to cleanse the atmosphere.

It takes a lot of energy to respond in anger. That response tends to deplete us and drain us. But if we use our energy to respond lovingly, we will not only bring harmony to the situation, we will be energized by that love. When we act lovingly, we are opening the door for God's love to flow through us. We are energized and boosted by godly love.

The next time we find ourselves in a situation in which an injustice is taking place, we can practice responding with love instead of anger. We can note the effect that our positive response has both on the situation and on our own well-being.

There is enough anger in the world. Let us bring harmony and peace to the world. Let us overcome violence with love. We will find the benefit of doing so will have a ripple effect and it will not be long before our environment, our community, and our society will become a haven of peace in this world.

Do Not Accept the Gift of Anger

A Brahman once invited Lord Buddha to come and have a meal at his home. Buddha agreed. When he arrived at the Brahman's house he found that the Brahman had invited him there for another purpose. The Brahman began to criticize him and abuse him.

The Buddha quietly listened to the Brahman's verbal attacks. This went on for some time.

Finally, the Buddha said, "Do visitors come to your home often, good Brahman?"

"Yes, they do," replied the Brahman.

Buddha continued, saying, "What preparations do you make for your guests when they come?"

The Brahman replied, "We get ready for a big feast."

The Buddha asked, "What happens if they do not arrive?"

The Brahman said, "We eat the food from the feast by ourselves."

The Buddha said, "Well, you have invited me for a meal but you entertained me with criticism and harsh words. It appears the feast you have prepared for me is abusive words. I do not want to eat from what you have prepared. So please take it back and eat it yourself." With that, the Buddha left the Brahman's house.

The Buddha realized that the feast that was given to him was not food, but verbal abuse. Rather than turning around, engaging in criticism, and abusing the Brahman in the same way, he refused to partake of the anger. Instead, he left the scene. Thus, the anger was left with the man who was giving it out.

The Buddha advised his disciples who were watching this whole scene, by saying, "Never retaliate in kind to what is done to you. Hatred never ends through more hatred."

Many times in life we are faced with people who say bad things to us, who verbally abuse us, who criticize us, and who call us names. Rather than engage at their level, we should not accept these gifts from others. Then their anger has nowhere to go. It remains with them. When we withdraw from the scene, they find themselves alone with their anger. Soon, they realize what they have done. They see how calm we were in the face of their poison. Sometimes they wonder how we were able to be loving in the face of their anger and they may come to respect us.

As we go about our day and are faced with people who are filled with anger and criticism toward us, we should look at their words calmly. We should ask first whether their words have any truth to them. If so, we can take their words as a lesson to improve ourselves. If their words do not have any truth to them, then we should not accept their gift of anger. We should not be dragged down to their level. In this way, we can maintain our equanimity and peacefulness. We add calmness to their hostile environment. We should leave the gift of anger with them and go on our peaceful, merry ways. In this way, we have kept our attention on our spiritual goals and we have become a positive influence in our environment.

Conquering Anger

One of the biggest threats to our peace of mind is the affliction of anger. At work, we often find ourselves angry at our boss, co-workers, or subordinates. Hardly a day goes by when someone or something at work does not disturb our peace of mind. We find that our homes are also a breeding ground for angry reactions. Someone did not pay a bill on time, someone else has gobbled up our favorite dessert, our children are arguing and giving us a headache, or our spouse made a commitment on our behalf that we would rather not keep. The list goes on and on. Even the trip to and from work stirs up our anger. Smooth-flowing traffic suddenly comes to a halt for no reason and we sit motionless for fifteen minutes. Someone does not let us change lanes and we miss our exit. Another driver cuts us off, nearly causing an accident. By the time we get to work, we are agitated and hostile.

It seems life is ready to pounce on us with another situation that stirs us to states of frenzy. Is there any antidote for anger? There is an instructive story from the Jain tradition that may give us insight on how to overcome anger.

There once were four princes: Vasudeva, Baladeva, Satyaka, and Daruka. One day, their headstrong horses carried them into a thick jungle. Since it was late, the four princes decided to sleep there for the night before returning home. They selected a large banyan tree under which they would rest. Since it was a dark jungle, they decided they needed to take turns standing watch. Thus, as three slept, one would stand guard to protect the others. After a while the guard would rest, and another prince would keep watch. Daruka was the first prince to stand watch. While the other three slept, anger disguised itself as a spirit and came to Daruka.

The spirit of anger said, "I am very hungry. I would like to eat your three sleeping companions."

Daruka said, "Nothing doing." He started fighting with the spirit of anger. A fierce battle ensued. When Daruka could not beat the spirit, he grew angry. The angrier Daruka became, the more energy the spirit of anger gained. With this renewed energy, anger finally struck Daruka and injured him on the leg. Daruka collapsed. The spirit of anger snuck away.

Next, the second prince, Satyaka, awoke because it was his turn to keep guard. As it was dark, he did not notice Daruka lying unconscious and injured. As Satyaka kept watch, the spirit of anger approached him, too. The same conversation transpired about anger wanting to eat Satyaka's companions. Satyaka began to fight with the spirit of anger, and as he could not overcome him, he also became angrier. This anger fueled the spirit of anger's fire and he gained strength. He struck Satyaka on the leg, and he too collapsed.

When it was time for the third prince, Baladeva, to keep watch, he faced the same situation. Anger thrived on Baladeva's anger and gained enough strength to attack him also.

Finally, it was time for Vasudeva to keep watch. The spirit of anger tried to play the same game with Vasudeva. "I want to eat your companions," said the spirit of anger.

Vasudeva replied, "I am sorry, but you cannot do so unless you defeat me." They too began fighting. Instead of becoming angry, Vasudeva merely appreciated how strong, courageous, and skillful the spirit was. Throughout the battle, Vasudeva remained calm. The calmer Vasudeva became, the more the spirit began losing strength. Finally, the spirit of anger was so weakened by Vasudeva's calm, that Vasudeva was able to defeat the spirit of anger, thus saving the other three princes.

When dawn came, Vasudeva could finally see what had happened. There lay each of his companions with broken bones. When he asked them who had done that to them, they explained that it was an evil spirit.

Vasudeva said, "It was the spirit of anger. All one needed to weaken its energy was to stay calm." He pointed to the spirit of anger that lay dead on the ground.

This is the secret to overcoming anger. The more we give in to anger, the angrier we become, and it gains its power over us. We reach a point in which we lose total control and end up doing or saying something that hurts others and ourselves.

To overcome anger, stay calm in the face of whatever is happening. As we face problems at home, at the office, or in traffic, we should not react in anger. We can recognize that the problems are there. We can take steps to solve the problem. We can even be proactive and try to re-move the agitating source by communication or by finding solutions, while trying to avoid becoming angry. Anger is not going to eliminate problems. All it will do is to make our own blood pressure go up, cause fight-or-flight hormones to circulate through our body and make us ill, and keep our mind in a state of obsessive agitation. The anger does not cause others to stop doing what they are doing. All anger does is make us sick and ineffective. But if we remain calm, we can tackle the problem with all our faculties fully in our control and we can find a more effective solution. We will have more energy to solve the problem.

What are the steps to overcome anger? First, when we feel ourselves getting angry we should not say or do anything immediately. Rather, we should take a deep breath and slow down. Then, we should sit in medita-tion. We should remove ourselves from the situation to be alone, and sit in a state of calm meditation. If angry thoughts try to intervene, we should ask ourselves whether we want to make the spirit of anger stronger or whether we wish to defeat it. If we wish to defeat it, then, like Vasudeva in the story, we can do so by not letting our anger feed the spirit of anger. We should realize that the longer we can remain calm, quiet, and composed, the less energy anger will have, and it will gradually vanish.

Let us destroy anger by our calmness, equipoise, and balance. We will find that while the same situations that incite us every day continue, we will not become slaves to them. We can calmly pass through them using our body, mind, and energy for more constructive purposes and then we will feel happier, more joyful, and more peaceful.

Gentleness Wins Over Force

The North Wind and the Sun once entered into a debate over who was more powerful and influential. The North Wind claimed that it was more powerful, while the Sun said that it was more powerful. They agreed to a contest. They said that whoever could make a person remove his coat would win. So they picked a man who was making his way home on a long trip by foot. The North Wind went first. It blew its wind hard to try to blow the man's coat off. It huffed and puffed. But the harder the wind blew, the more intently the man wrapped his coat tightly around himself. The North Wind tried for a long time to get the man to take his coat off, but it did not work. Next, the Sun had its turn. It began to send warm, loving rays upon the man. Steadily, the sun beat down its warmth. After a while the man began to feel warm. He unbuttoned his coat. The sun continued to shine on him. Finally, the man felt warm enough and took off his coat.

With a smile, the Sun said to the North Wind, "As you can see, my warm, loving ways made him remove his coat, while your strong, forceful ways caused him to resist."

Aesop's fable teaches a valuable lesson. Love and gentleness always win out over force. Some people feel that they can get the best out of others by being forceful, harsh, and critical. Hardly anyone responds to such treatment. We feel that we have to treat others harshly or forcefully to get them to do anything. Yet, quite the opposite is true. We can be more persuasive, using the power of love and gentleness. People get discouraged when they are spoken to harshly or abruptly. They shut down and want to withdraw. But when people are given loving and encouraging words and are spoken to sweetly, they want to go out of their way to do more.

Adding honey to life makes the world more loving. Adding the warmth of love makes things go more smoothly. If we can be like the Sun, and send warm, encouraging words and smiles to others, we will find that we can be more effective in whatever we do. Being forceful does not work in the long run.

It is the same with our meditations. When we try to force the results, they seem to elude us more and more. When we sit lovingly and sweetly in meditation, then the results can come on their own. We should avoid clutching. We should do our work in meditation effortlessly and lovingly and then the grace of God can flow.

Let us learn a lesson from the Sun. Let us act lovingly and gently with others. Let us also be loving and gentle with our meditations and wait for the fruits to appear.

Do Your Best

Give Your Best to Everyone

A long time ago, a band of musicians made their living by traveling from one town to another, performing their music. Times were hard and they were not earning much money. The poor people who used to come to hear them could no longer afford the small fee they charged for their music. Attendance was steadily dropping until only a few people were turning out to hear the performances.

One day, the group met to decide what to do.

One said, "I see no reason for performing tonight with so few people coming."

Another one noticed that snow had started to fall and said, "Look! Who will come out tonight with the snow falling like this?"

A third added, "Yes, last night we had very few people. If it snows like this tonight, even fewer will come. Let's return their small fees and cancel."

The first agreed and said, "You are right. No one can expect us to keep playing when only a few are in the audience."

The second one said, "Yes. Who can expect anyone to do his or her best for just a few?"

The fourth musician had been sitting silently, listening to the conversation. The others turned to him and said, "What do you think?"

He said, "I know you are discouraged. I am also discouraged. But we have a responsibility to those who come. We will continue to play, and we will do the best job we can at all times. It is not the fault of those who come that others do not come. They should not be punished by our giving less than we can give."

The other musicians felt encouraged by his words and decided to play that night. They gave one of the best performances of their lives.

When the show was over and everyone had left, the fourth musician called the troupe together and handed them a note. He said, "One of the audience members left this note for us before the doors closed behind him." He opened the note and it read: "Thank you for a beautiful performance tonight." The note was signed "Your King."

This story serves to illustrate some important points. The decision to play their best happened to fall on the night that the king surprised them with an appearance. Yet they had decided to give their best to whoever came. This is an attitude with which we should always work. It is an attitude of realizing that all have the king in them. Everyone is important. We all have the soul in us and we are all a part of God. When we work with an attitude that every person deserves the best we can give, we are honoring the God within everyone.

Some people only work hard to please certain people. They may give their best for their boss, or for the rich, or for someone who can do a favor for them. But great are the people who do their best for the poor, or for those who have nothing to give them. Great are the people who treat all equally well.

Another lesson is that we should not be discouraged when we do something and it seems that only a few are appreciating us or benefiting from us. It is said that if we can transform even one life, our life is worth living. When we make an effort and the expected crowds do not turn up, we are still being of help to others, even if only one or two show up. We should never feel that it is not worth doing something we had planned if only a few people show up. We are making a difference in those people's lives. If we work hard and only a few people partake of what we have done, it is important for those people. We should not give up in discouragement. The musicians played for only a few, but one of them turned out to be the king.

Everything we do is seen by God. We should always do and give our best. The reward is in the service, not the fruits of the service. If we live in this way, we will go to bed each night with the satisfaction of knowing that we have given our all. We will be blessed with the joy and bliss from within that come from giving our best to everyone we meet.

Contentment

Desire and Contentment

We are all craving peace. No one wants turmoil. Let us examine this instructive story and see what we can learn about the way to peace.

One day, Desire and Contentment got into a hot debate over which of them was greater than the other. This argument went on and on, until they finally decided to seek a wise man—as is done in most tales—to help them settle the dispute.

They headed off for the mountaintop, where most wise men in the old tales lived. The wise man listened to their arguments and said, "To prove which of you is right, I want you both to take turns living with a rich and happy man. After both of you have lived with the man, we will let him make the decision as to which one of you is greater."

Desire and Contentment thought that was a fair way to decide the issue. So, they descended the mountain to the village below to find a rich and happy man with whom to live. They decided that Desire should live with the man first.

As soon as Desire moved into the man's home, the rich and happy man found that his normally calm and just mind was filled with evil thoughts. One day, the man suddenly said to his wife, "Let us leave our home and take a journey throughout the world. I want to visit many far-off and exotic places." The wife looked at him as if he had gone mad. Finally, after much persuasion, the man got his wife to agree to go with him. The man emptied his bank account and purchased expensive tickets on boats to travel across the seas and to stay at expensive hotels.

"You are wasting much of your money," cried the wife throughout their journey. However, the man was filled with so many desires to see this place and that place and to buy this expensive souvenir and that memento.

When they returned home from the trip, the man discovered that he had run out of money. Thus, he had to start several businesses to gain the money back. He found himself working day and night for the money. All the leisure time he had when he was wealthy was gone, and he found he had to work long hours. The result of this hard work was that he could not stay ahead of his competition, and he ended up losing most of his money.

One day, fed up with his new houseguest named Desire, he told him, "You have been the source of all my trouble. Get out of here. I don't want you around anymore." Desire, fearing for his life, rushed out of the house, into the waiting arms of Contentment.

Contentment, grinning from ear to ear, said, "So, things are not going so well for you, are they?"

Desire said, "Well, if you think you are so great, then you try living with that man. I don't think you would do any better, for he is hot-tempered."

Contentment entered the house of the man and made itself at home. The minute Contentment entered, the man uttered a deep sigh of relief. Suddenly, the man was filled with renewed hope and strength. The man went to work in a calm way. Joy filled his heart. His wife noticed this sudden change in him. He had returned to the happy, just man that he was before Desire entered his life.

The man turned to Contentment and said, "Your company makes me so happy. I hope that I am never separated from you."

Contentment peeped out of the window at Desire and smiled, for he had won the debate.

If we track the route of any desire, we can see what kind of troubles to which it often leads. They may be large or small tribulations, but they cause a disturbance in our sea of tranquility. Let us say we want to buy something expensive. We either have to work harder to get it, thus taking away from our leisure and free time, or we have to give up something else for it. We may have to sell our favorite old car to buy a new, larger one. We may have to deny ourselves something else we want, to fulfill another desire. Some people are so desperate to buy something they want that they may even resort to dishonest means such as cheating, taking money from their loved ones, or even stealing.

Maybe we desire something that is not an object. We may crave power over others. That too is a treacherous road. We have to step over many people, lie, deceive, and manipulate others to get what we want. Others will grow wise to us, and in response will either avoid us, defame us, or attack us. There is no end to the troubles such a person faces when he or she tries to gain control over everyone and everything.

If we want fame, we may have to publicize ourselves to all we meet. Our ego gets inflated. Look at how some people have to deceive, lie, and make false promises to get people to join their bandwagon. Actors and actresses have to bear the scandalous news articles about them to get publicity. The fame they thought they wanted is often laden with a scandalous reputation.

There is no end to the desires of the mind and to the troubles to which they lead. Once we start out on the road of desire, we become like the rich man in the story. We wonder why we left our safe haven of peace and contentment to have to bear all these trials and tribulations. In the end, we start craving the peace and contentment we had before desire led us astray.

If we want peace and happiness, let us resist giving in to all the desires of our mind, and instead honor the contentment that is ours in the depths of our soul.

As we meditate, let us bar the door from the never-ending desires knocking to get in. Instead, sit in the sanctuary of our soul in a state of peace and contentment, safe from the troubles that desires bring.

Which Race Are We Running?

There is an instructive story from the writing of Leo Tolstoy. There was a peasant in Russia who owned a small plot of land. He led a life of peace and contentment until one day he began to envy his brother-in-law who was a rich landlord. He watched as his brother-in-law bought more and more land and had more and more tenants. The more prosperous he grew, the more the peasant began desiring to do the same. He started saving his money to buy some land.

When the peasant had raised enough capital, he started looking for land to buy. He heard there was some cheap land in a neighboring territory. When he traveled to see the land, he found that the people living on it lived a nomadic life.

The peasant brought some gifts for the chief in charge of that territory. The chief thanked him for the gifts and said he could have as much land as he could walk around before sunset. The agreement was that he start out in the morning and whatever distance he could walk by sunset, the peasant could keep the land.

The peasant was overjoyed at the possibility of owning such a great amount of land. The villagers gathered to watch his race against time. He started out walking extremely fast so he could cover more ground. When the sun was high in the sky it became extremely hot. But the peasant did not want to waste time stopping for food and water lest he miss out on some more land. He thought if he kept going, he would get more land. The peasant was trying to cover the largest area he could by walking in a large circle, which ended up being a long distance.

He grew so greedy and ambitious that as the sun became hotter and hotter, he refused to stop for water. His legs grew more and more tired, but he refused to take rest even for a few moments. Finally, the sun was about to set. The crowd began to applaud his victory. As he returned to the starting point, exhaustion and thirst overcame him to the point that he collapsed. Before the crowd realized what had transpired, he had died of exhaustion and thirst.

Sadly, the people prepared for his funeral. They buried him on the same spot on which he collapsed. Thus, the only land he needed was the six feet by four feet of land in which his body would be buried.

This sad story of greed is not much different from the lives of many people on earth. What do most people do? They spend their lives in a race to try to make as much money as they can, accumulate as much land and as many possessions as they can, make as great a name for themselves as they can, or gain as much power as they can, only to find the race ends at their time of death.

Few people find contentment and peace in their lives when they live to gather only material gains in this world. People think a time will come when they will finally have enough so they can sit back and enjoy the fruits of their labor. But too many end up leaving the world before they can find that peace.

The world is like a race. Some call it a rat race. We run around on a treadmill or wheel going nowhere fast. Before we know it, the whistle blows and the time of the race is up.

The peasant was content until he began to envy what others had. Then he began a race that ended in his demise.

Few realize that contentment and peace are ours for the asking. They are already inside us. If we can be still and tap within, we will find riches far greater than any available on earth. We do not need to exert to find them. We can go about our daily life, earning our honest livelihood, providing for our families, and making enough to share with others, and still enjoy the peace and contentment within ourselves. We need not sacrifice that inner peace in the pursuit of outer riches which may or may not come or which may or may not provide the happiness we think it will give us.

The peasant did not take even a moment for rest and drink. Similarly, do we take moments in our lives for spiritual retreat, rest, and a drink from the fountain of Light within us? There is a fountainhead of bliss, love, and peace within us. Do we ever take a moment to stop and drink from it?

Let us not be like the peasant. Let us find time each day to stop and refresh ourselves in the fountain of divine treasures within by spending time in meditation. In this way, we can quench our thirst with the love of God that will fill us with love and peace as we go about our daily life. We will reach our worldly goals with peace and calm, and we will be overflowing with the inner bliss that makes our life beautiful.

No End to Desires

Once upon a time there was a carpenter who worked out of his home. Every day he took joy in building some furniture or tools to sell to others. He merrily sang and hummed as he worked, content with life.

One day, his rich neighbor grew fed up with the noise the carpenter made as he hammered the wood. The neighbor had reached a point in which he could not take the noise anymore. The neighbor finally had a plan to quiet the carpenter. He took several hundred dollars from his money and left it in an envelope in the carpenter's workshop. The neighbor thought if he gave the carpenter money he would not have to work and he would stop his incessant hammering.

The carpenter entered his workshop and found the envelope lying there. Instead of using it to take a vacation or a break, the carpenter thought, "Someone left me several hundred dollars. What good fortune! I will take some of the money and invest in new tools so I can build bigger and better furniture and make more money." Thus, the money flamed the carpenter's desire to earn more money. He began working even harder, hoping to increase the newly found hundreds into thousands.

As he began to make more money, he was still not content. He decided he wanted to turn the thousands into tens of thousands, and thus he worked still harder. The rich neighbor was annoyed that his plan had failed, and instead of silencing the carpenter, it merely increased the noise because now the man worked longer hours.

When the carpenter had earned tens of thousands he wanted to make a hundred thousand. He put pressure upon himself to work day and night and even on weekends. Soon, he stopped his humming and singing. He no longer took joy in his work, but felt strangled by the pressure he had put upon himself. On many nights, he was so stressed out he could not even sleep. The inner contentment and peace he had when he was just a poor carpenter were gone in the pursuit of trying to make more and more money.

Consider our own lives. Do we find ourselves spending all of our time working to make money so we can retire? Do we work overtime to make more money? Do we work all weekend long to increase our profits? Do we find that we cannot even take a day or even several hours off work without thinking about our work? If this is what is happening to us, are we becoming like the carpenter? If we make all the money in the world but cannot enjoy personal peace and joy in our work, is it worth it?

If we find that we are devoting too much of our time to making money and not enough to our family, our hobbies, our spiritual pursuits, and those things we love, then we need to analyze whether we are making the right choices. It is good to save for the future, but is it worth using up our entire life in trying to have more than what we need?

Who knows what the future will bring? When we become old, will we have the health to do what we waited our whole life to do? If we leave our spiritual pursuits until we have reached our senior years, who knows how much time we will have left or whether we will be able to devote time to spirituality at that stage. If we ignore our family until they are already grown and have children of their own, we miss an important part of their lives that can never be recovered.

Let us consider how we spend our time. If we have decided that certain goals are important, then we should try to find time for them throughout our life, and not put them all on the back burner in the pursuit of amassing more money than we need. We should weigh our time and make sure that we do not lose our peace and contentment over the stress of being engaged in a mad pursuit for money and possessions. Being conscious of how we spend our time and our life is important. If we listen to our soul, we will find that inner peace and contentment are more valuable than all the riches in the world.

)X(

Acceptance

"Whatever You Give Me Tastes Sweet"

In our daily life we face many difficulties, hardships, and disappointments. Things do not always go our way. If we listen to the discussions of others and review our own words and thoughts, we find that many of them deal with complaints about how life is treating us. Life seems to be bitter at times, and in turn makes us bitter.

Have we ever thought about life from a different perspective? Think about how fortunate we really are. After all, we are human beings. How many species of life are there that walk the earth? There are mammals, reptiles, and insects. There are creatures of the air and creatures of the sea. Fortunately for us, we have been born as human beings.

How many of us have ever thanked God for the life we have been given? We complain to God when things go wrong, but what about the hundreds of things that God has given us? God has provided us enough food to keep us alive this long. We have had protection from the elements in the form of clothes and some sort of shelter. Most of us have families who love us. We have received some kind of education and have some kind of work.

If we take all that comes to us as a gift from God, then we can accept the good and the tribulations equally under God's will. In this respect, there is a story about King Mahmud of Ghazni. One day, while he was sitting with his most devoted servant, Ayaz, he shared half of his cucumber with him. Ayaz thanked him and happily ate the piece given to him by the king. When he had finished, the king then took a bite of his own half.

"Yuk!" he cried, as he made a disgusted face, and spit out the cucumber. "This is so bitter! How could you have eaten your piece if it tasted like bitter poison?"

Ayaz replied, "My dear king, I have enjoyed so many favors and blessings from you all these years. Whatever you give me tastes sweet!"

Ayaz's attitude demonstrates the frame of mind of a true lover of God. Such a lover is so much enamored of God and so grateful to God, that he or she takes everything, good or bitter, as a gift of the Beloved. Ayaz had received so many blessings from the king that he felt it was not his place to complain if one of these gifts was bitter. After all, if the king gave him so much good, he must love him. If therefore, once in a blue moon, he handed him something bitter, Ayaz knew he had no evil intention. He accepted all the king gave him with love and gratitude.

If we could accept the rainy days with the same gratitude as we do the sunny days, we would find our lives would be more full of love, peace, and happiness. If we could appreciate the weeds as well as the roses, we would enrich our daily lives. If we could appreciate our enemies as well as our friends, we would not have to waste precious breaths in complaints and bitterness. If we could accept days when we are ill and under the weather as well as those in which we are well and healthy, we would reduce our stress and worry, and maybe even heal faster.

Life is precious. Do we want to live our lives to their fullest? The pain and disappointments will not go away by complaining about them. We must pass through those times. Let us try to do so in a state of calm acceptance and conserve the energy that we normally use for complaining. Instead we can think of God in love and gratitude. We will find that we pass through the times of tribulations more easily.

Like Ayaz, let us take everything coming from God as tasting sweet. Then, we will sweeten our whole lives and the lives of those around us.

Success and Reaching Goals

Being One-pointed

Success in any field requires us to be one-pointed. Whether we wish to become a doctor, an Olympic athlete, a great singer, an artist, or a wealthy businessperson, we need to be totally focused in achieving the goal. Look at the life of anyone who has made a great accomplishment. One finds that he or she had a ruling passion for a goal.

It is no different in the realm of spiritual development. It is important to be one-pointed in our attention when we do our spiritual practices. Our ruling passion should be on the realization of our true self.

There is a story from the life of a great Sufi saint, Bayazid Bistami. Once, Bistami was sitting with his spiritual teacher. The teacher asked Bistami to bring him a book lying near the window.

Bistami replied, "What window? Where is there a window?"

The teacher was amazed and said, "How is it that you have been coming to see me all these years and do not know where the window is?"

The disciple replied, "What do I care about the windows? When I am with you, I see only you. I do not gaze at anything else but you."

The teacher smiled and said, "You can return home now. Your course of spiritual study with me is complete! You have reached the goal!"

When trying to find our soul and God, we should focus on finding them and nothing else. When we are communing with God, we should not be aware of anything else. We should drink deeply from the intoxication of God and let it fill us up and uplift us. When in meditation, we should concentrate into the middle of the Light that we see before us and ignore any thoughts that arise. When listening to the inner Sound of God, we should stay focused on the Sound and ignore any distracting thoughts that arise. In this way, we too, like the disciple in the story, will complete the course of our spiritual studies and find our cherished goal.

We should sit in meditation and prayer with one-pointed concentration. We should not let anything interfere with our attention. We should not notice anything else in our surroundings. While in meditation, we should not pay attention to the world outside or our body below. We should not pay any attention to our thoughts. We should sit at the door as if we were one big eye and wait with loving devotion for whatever comes to us. This is the way to achieve success on the spiritual path.

Regularity

People want inner experiences in their meditations. Yet, most of them hardly put in any time to meditate. Succeeding at anything in life takes regularity and practice.

To illustrate this, there is the story of the rain and the rock. Once the earth, the wind, and the rain were talking to a large rock. The rock said, "I am stronger than all of you put together."

At first, the three of them agreed that the rock was very strong. But suddenly, the rain said, "You may be strong, but I am more powerful than you."

The others laughed at the rain.

"How could you be more powerful than a rock? You are merely small drops of water."

The rain said, "I can put a hole in the rock if I want to."

Everyone laughed at the rain and thought he must be delusional.

"Just watch and see," said the rain.

And so the rain began to fall. Small, steady drops beat against the rock.

Days passed and nothing happened.

"You have been raining on the rock for days," said the wind, "and nothing has happened. There is no hole in the rock."

The rain said, "Do not worry. Watch and see."

Months passed and the rain kept beating on the rock. Finally, after several years, the wind and earth heard a scream. They rushed to the rock.

"What is wrong?" they asked.

"The rain has been coming down so steadily all these years, that a hole has formed in me." Sure enough, the raindrops had cut a hole in the rock.

"How did you do that?" the others asked the rain.

"It is not by violent cutting of the rock that the hole has been formed, but by my falling steadily and regularly on the rock," said the rain.

This story teaches us how to have spiritual progress within. Inner experiences do not come by a sudden effort. They come by gentle and steady effort, day after day, over time. It is by steady practice that we make progress. As the adage goes, "Slow and steady wins the race."

If we think that by meditating six hours once a year we will attain our goal, we are mistaken. It is by spending some time daily, day after day, that we will make the pathway into the Beyond.

Let us be regular. Let us find time each day to meditate. Then, like the steady rain, drop by drop, bit by bit, we will gradually enter the world of Light.

Making the Best Use of One's Time

There is a legendary story about a poor wood-cutter. He worked hard to earn his livelihood. One day, as the king was passing through the wood-cutter's part of the woods he saw the man working hard. He felt sorry for the man's poverty and wanted to do something to help him.

"Woodcutter," said the king, "I have some land with some sandalwood trees on it. I will give you that land so you can use it to become rich."

The woodcutter thanked him. Since he did not realize the value of the sandalwood trees, after cutting them down he sold them for the same price as the regular trees. After he had used most of the trees, the king returned. Expecting to see the man rich, the king was shocked to find him still in poverty.

"How is it that you have not made any money from selling the sandalwood trees?" inquired the king. "Those trees are worth a lot of money."

The woodcutter realized that he had lost a golden opportunity. There were but a few trees left. He was able to sell those for the correct value and earn enough to live on comfortably.

The story of the woodcutter is the story of our life. The sandalwood is equivalent to the number of breaths we have been given in our life. But, like the woodcutter, we waste much of the precious gift of our breath and our time. Instead of amassing spiritual riches with our gift, we are wasting away our time. Time is precious. Once it is gone we cannot retrieve it. Let us make the best use of our time. If we do so, then we can amass spiritual wealth far beyond our wildest dreams.

There is a saying that helps to remind us about the importance of every moment. For what are we trading away that moment? Do we want to trade it away for thoughts of anger or greed? Do we want to trade it away to brood over the past or worry about the future? Do we want to spend it on pastimes that have no value for us? Or do we wish to spend the moment in doing something to discover who we really are and why we are here? What will be the most valuable for us in our life?

Are we aimlessly adrift on the sea of life? Do we spend some time in our life to decide the direction in which we wish to go? Sant Kirpal Singh Ji Maharaj, my spiritual Master, spent time in his early years deciding what he wanted to do with his life. After much soul-searching, he finally decided, "God first, and the world next." He took the decision that he wanted to attain self-knowledge and God-realization as his first priority. With that goal in mind, his course was set, and he did not stop until he reached his goal.

If we look at the lives of great people, we find many of these people had decided a direction in life. They may have wished to pursue their art, their hobby, their science, their research, or their spiritual growth, but they all held one thing in common. They were not aimlessly adrift; they had a course set and they followed it.

Tegh Bahadur, the ninth Guru of the Sikhs, spent years meditating in a small closet room until he found God. Lord Buddha left his kingdom to search for enlightenment. He spent years finding answers to questions about the nature of the world and who we really are. Prophet Mohammed spent many years in a cave in pursuit of Allah.

If we wish to discover our soul, we need to allot time to it. We have seen how easily our life can be eaten away by just trying to keep our physical body alive and cared for. Activities like eating, sleeping, dressing, and working to make money to pay for our necessities in life occupy a good portion of our time. With little time left over, we want to evaluate how to make the best use of it. Like the woodcutter, we do not want to throw away the precious gift of time in our human existence.

We can analyze how much time we devote to various activities throughout the twenty-four hours of the day. Then we can decide how to fit in time for finding our soul within us. To uncover the luminosity and riches of our soul, we need to spend time daily in meditation. The more time we can put in for this quest, the better. If we spend time daily in the quiet of our own self and tap our spiritual divinity within us, then we will use the gift of the sandalwood trees to its full benefit and will have made the best use of our life.

Failure Leads to Success

Thomas Edison was the inventor of the lightbulb. We can well imagine what our lives would be like if it were not for this marvelous invention. The lightbulb makes it possible for us to utilize the night for those activities that through the ages were mostly possible only in the day. Candlelight and fires have a limited lighting capacity.

While we may take this invention for granted, it was invented through relentless labor. It is said that one day, a critic tried to belittle Edison by saying that Edison had failed 25,000 times while experimenting with a storage battery.

The great Edison replied, "No, I did not fail. I discovered 24,999 ways that the storage battery does not work."

Edison's persistence produced wonderful inventions. His attitude toward failure was what made him successful. He looked upon failure as a learning experience leading him closer to success. Had he given up on the first, the tenth, the hundredth, or the 24,999th try, he never would have succeeded.

We can apply Edison's attitude toward failure to our own spiritual life, including our practice of prayer and meditation. Many sit for meditation and prayer day after day, and sometimes feel discouraged if they have not reached their spiritual goal by the tenth time they meditate. Instead of pursuing our goals and persisting in our meditation, many people give up. They feel that if they did not attain their goal right away, they have failed. This attitude causes them to give up too early. If Edison put in the time to keep designing a lightbulb 25,000 times until he succeeded, couldn't we sit for meditation 25,000 times to turn on the inner lightbulb?

Failure should not discourage us. If we sit for meditation and receive some flashes of light, or some colors of lights, we should not be disappointed. These are first steps. By sitting regularly, we will become more proficient in our meditations. We have no idea how beneficial every minute spent in meditation is for us. We may not see the progress right away, but all the minutes and hours we spend in meditation have a cumulative effect. If we give up because one day we do not see anything, and another day we see a pinpoint of light, and a third day we see some blue light, then we may not see the great day when we are filled with the effulgent Light of our destination.

Being like Edison takes persistence. This means taking each day we think we have failed as if it were a lesson on what *not* to do in our meditation. If we have a day without Light in our meditation, it is a time to analyze if we have not done the technique correctly. Were we busy thinking about the past or the future instead of meditating? Each failure is a chance to improve next time. We will learn the 24,999 things *not to do* in our meditation. By the 25,000th time we may finally discover the right way to meditate and suddenly be blessed with showers upon showers of radiant Light.

As we sit for meditation and prayer, let us not to be discouraged. We should do our part to meditate accurately, and leave the rest to God. Then, one day, we will find that all our efforts have borne fruit, and we will discover the switch to keep the lightbulb within glowing eternally.

Diligent Commitment to Our Life's Goal

If we look at the lives of saints and Masters through the ages, we find one quality that was critical to their success. It was not that they were born with superhuman abilities. It was not that they were more than human. The quality that set them apart was a diligent commitment to their life's spiritual goal. They set their eyes upon their stars and did not stop until they reached their goal. If we wish to attain any goal in life, the secret to success is to stick to that goal through rain or shine, or through smooth-sailing or rough waters. This is true whether we wish to attain a spiritual goal or a worldly achievement. Even people who attained worldly goals in sports, the sciences, or the arts have accomplished wonders through a firm commitment to their goal.

In this connection, we have an anecdote from the life of the great Indian writer, poet, and thinker, Rabindranath Tagore. He established the ashram Shantiniketan and would work hard there every day. Once, Mahatma Gandhi, while visiting him there in 1939, gave a public talk. After the talk he spent time with Rabindranath Tagore, sharing topics of interest to both of them. After lunch, Gandhi Ji went to take rest when some of the ashram workers who were followers of Rabindranath Tagore approached him.

"Can you help us, Gandhi Ji?" they asked.

"What is it?" asked Mahatma Gandhi.

"We are worried about the health of Rabindranath Tagore. He is not keeping good health. The doctors advised him to take rest, but he refuses. After lunch, he immediately goes back to work and does not take a moment's rest. We do not want his health to fail."

Gandhi Ji asked, "Why do you want me to tell him?"

They said, "We know he will not go against your advice." So Gandhi Ji agreed to try to talk to Rabindranath Tagore about taking some rest.

After Gandhi Ji had had his rest, he went to Tagore's residence. He saw that Tagore was deeply immersed in his work. When Tagore looked up and saw Gandhi Ji there he asked him, "Are you not comfortable here that you have come out from your rest so soon?"

Gandhi Ji said, "I have come to ask something of you. Please grant it to me without knowing what it is."

Tagore said, "I must know what it is first."

"Fine," said Gandhi Ji, "I have come to ask you to take rest after your lunch so your health does not fail. You are not keeping fit these days."

Tagore replied, "How can I do that? I must tell you the truth so that you will understand. When I was twelve I put on the sacred thread. At that ceremony, I took a vow never to rest at any time during the day for any reason. Up to now I have kept that vow. How many more years do I have to live? Why would I break that vow now?"

Tagore's firm determination and commitment to his promise moved Gandhi Ji. For sixty-seven years, Tagore had never rested in the day. Gandhi Ji was impressed by his commitment to his goal.

Gandhi Ji then told him, "Now I know the secret of your success!"

If someone can make a commitment to a worldly goal and achieve great success as Tagore had done, imagine what one could do in the spiritual realms. If we could commit to our meditation with the same firm determination as Tagore had done to his writing and worldly work, we too would be successful. The trouble is not that we are incapable of spiritual progress — because that gift is available to each — but that we lack commitment. On one day we meditate a few minutes, then for the next few days we do not meditate at all, and then we meditate an hour on a following day, and maybe every so often we put in long hours on a special day. That is not true commitment. That is only a half-hearted attempt. But if we were to put in regular time faithfully every day, we would find the progress we seek.

For those who truly wish spiritual progress, it is possible by a firm commitment to the goal. If we could make the commitment once and for all and stick to it as diligently as did Tagore toward his worldly goal, we would be soaring into the inner spiritual planes.

Letting Go

Clutching and Letting Go

Once upon a time, there was a man who lived alone. He kept his money in a special jar so that no one could steal it. One day, while the man was out farming his land, a thief broke into his house. Looking for something to steal, he came across a heavy stone jar. He could barely jiggle it to hear the coins inside. He could not lift the jar. So the man stuck his hand in the jar to take out the money. His hand fit perfectly into the jar.

The man grabbed as much money as he could, holding it in his fist. But when he tried to pull out his hand, it would not come out. He tried his hardest to pull out his hand, but the fist made his hand wider. While holding the money, he could not get it through the neck of the jar. He let go of the money and his hand was freed to come out of the jar. But he was intent upon having the money, so he tried again and again. Each time he enclosed the coins in his fist, his hand was too wide to be removed from the jar.

Suddenly, he heard the owner coming home. He knew that if he did not get his hand out of the jar, he would be caught. But he was so intent upon trying to get the money out that he would not give up. The result was that the man came in, caught him, and had him arrested.

We too are like the thief in the story. Desires cause us to be caught with our hand in the jar. Desires keep us bound to this world. It is only by letting go of the things of this world that we can be free. We need to stop clutching for whatever binds us as prisoners of our desires so we can enjoy true freedom. We need to stop clutching and let go. Then we will find the joy of freedom.

What kind of joy did the thief have in his pursuit of the money? Instead he ended up a prisoner in the jail. We too are like prisoners in the jail of this physical world. We spend all our time going after things that will not give us happiness. Whatever material gains we have in the world can lead us to more bondage if we are attached to them. For example, if we want a big house, we have to work longer hours to make enough money to pay for its mortgage. Then we need to fill it up with more and more furniture. That will take more time to work to pay for it, shop to buy it, and then to clean and repair everything. Before we know it, the house that was supposed to bring us pleasure has made us a slave to it. We no longer have time for our family, our children, or pursuits that will give us more fulfillment. We spend all our time going after things that may not give us true and lasting happiness.

Similarly, we may want to buy a computer to keep up with the latest technology. We then find ourselves working harder to buy all the right software and equipment to make it work. Soon we realize that we are not happy with a simple computer. We want to upgrade to a faster and more elaborate computer. Next, we find the computer that was supposed to save us time is taking up all our time. We end up spending hours learning to use the computer. We spend hours exploring the Internet. The e-mail system that was supposed to make communications faster is taking more and more of our time. Suddenly, we find fifty people e-mailing us daily and they expect an instantaneous response. If we do not respond right away they accuse us of being nonresponsive and indifferent. Soon, we are spending hours on the computer. We have become slaves to our possessions.

How can we end our bondage? We need to let go and be free. When we can let go of our desires for impermanent gains, we can be free. Then, our soul can experience the love and beauty that God has to offer. True happiness comes when we connect with the source of joy within us — our soul and God. To do so, we must turn our attention from the worldly enticements and listen to our soul. Beautiful melodies of God are playing within us all the time. Light and love are shining within us. By turning our attention from the world, we are releasing our hold on the coins that keep our hand stuck in the jar. By letting go, we are gaining eternal freedom.

By sitting in meditation, free from all worldly desires and attachments, we can let go and find ourselves free to soar back to God.

Perseverance

Perseverance Leads to Success

One of Aesop's fables tells about an old crow. The crow was wandering in the wilderness and became thirsty. He had not had anything to drink in days. Finally, he found a jug that had a little bit of water in the bottom. The bird reached its beak into the jug to drink, but the beak could not touch the bottom. At first he did not know what to do. It seemed he was not going to be able to drink the water. Then he had an idea. He started dropping in small pebbles, one at a time. As each pebble was dropped in, the water at the bottom rose a bit. One by one he added more and more pebbles. For a while it seemed useless because he still could not reach the water. But after enough pebbles were put in, the water rose up and the bird could drink it and satisfy his thirst.

This situation is similar to the time we spend in meditation. It may seem like each hour is going nowhere and we are not making progress. But we cannot see the results in the early stages. Finally, those hours of sustained, accurate meditation will suddenly accumulate and we will find we start making enormous gains in our meditation.

    We should not be discouraged and we should definitely not give up. We should persevere in our meditations, and one day, to our surprise, the water of spirituality will rise up and we can drink from it to our heart's content.

Optimism

Find Good in Everything

Many tend to see a half-filled glass as half empty rather than half full. When looking at a situation, the popular tendency is to think about the bad side rather than the good.

There is an instructive story regarding the character in literature known as Robinson Crusoe. He was stranded on a desert island and had to find a way to survive.

While he was on the island he made two lists. One list he called "evil" and one he called "good." He thought over his situation and he entered what was happening to him into one of the two columns. This is what he wrote:

"I am stranded on the desert island, which is bad. But I am still alive, which is good. The rest of the people on the ship died, but I survived."

Next, he wrote, "I am all alone, which is bad. But I am not starving, which is good."

As he thought further about his situation he wrote, "I have no clothes, which is bad. But, on the other hand, it is so hot here that I do not need clothes, so that is good."

Then he wrote, "I have no weapons to defend myself against animals, which is bad. But there are no wild animals along this beach here, so that is good."

Finally he wrote, "I have no one to talk to, which is bad. But the ship is near the shore and I can get things from the ship for my basic needs, which is good."

After going over his list, Robinson Crusoe decided that there was no situation so terrible that humans could not find a reason to have gratitude to God. There was a silver lining in everything.

This attitude is a healthy one and saves a lot of time being anxious, worried, depressed, and disheartened. This time can be used instead to find God, by staying focused on our spiritual goal. Every time we complain and fret over our situation, we are wasting valuable time.

Two people may go to the same party. One may spend time finding fault with all the people there, complaining about the food, and feeling upset that his or her expectations were not met. Another person may find enjoyment in being with the other people and selecting food from the buffet that he or she enjoys. Both are in the same environment. One is finding what is wrong and the other is looking for what is good and joyous. When they both leave the party one will say he or she had a terrible time, and the other will say he or she had a great time. Which one will feel more uplifted and buoyant at the end of the party?

Similarly, each day we face many situations. We can choose to focus on the bad and spend the rest of our time complaining and being disappointed, or we can choose to focus on what is good and take joy and pleasure from it.

We can develop spiritually by keeping our attention on being positive and occupying our time with spiritual thoughts. If we choose to occupy ourselves with negative thoughts that rattle around our head, we will waste valuable time that could be spent on remembering God.

Find some good in everything. Even when faced with challenges, we can think of the bright side and make the best use of our precious human life.

Selfless Service

God Blesses Those Who Give

One of the greatest things a human being can do is to give of himself or herself to serve others. Sant Kirpal Singh Ji Maharaj used to say, "Give, give, and give." Many people fear giving because they worry that they will have less. They do not realize there is a law of abundance at work in the universe. Whenever we give selflessly, unasked for, we end up having more.

There is a wonderful anecdote to illustrate this. Once there was an elderly man from Arabia. He had three sons. When he was nearing his end, he called his sons to his deathbed and told them, "When I die, you are to divide my belongings."

He turned to his oldest son and said, "I want you to take half of my worldly possessions."

Next, he turned to his middle son and said, "I want you to have one third of my belongings."

Finally, he told his youngest son, "You shall have one ninth of my worldly belongings."

Shortly thereafter, the elderly man died. When an account was taken of his possessions, it was discovered that all he owned were seventeen camels. The sons began to discuss dividing up the seventeen animals.

Soon they discovered that it was impossible to divide the camels exactly as their father had asked. They began to fight among themselves about their shares. Not knowing what to do, they went to an elderly friend of their father for advice.

The friend realized that the seventeen camels could not be divided into a half, a third, and a ninth. He thought for a while and said, "I am poor. I own only one camel. But if I add that camel to your herd, you can divide the camels according to your father's wishes and have harmony among yourselves.

When he added his camel to the seventeen, there were eighteen camels, which could easily be divided as the boys' father wished. To the eldest he gave one half, which turned out to be nine camels. To the middle son, he gave one third, which turned out to be six camels. To the youngest he gave one ninth of eighteen, which turned out to be two camels. The boys left happily.

When the elderly friend turned around, he realized that lo and behold his own camel remained! He thanked God, saying, "O God, Your wisdom surpasses all understanding!"

This story illustrates that we never lose when we give. The elderly man was so selfless he was willing to give his only possession away for the dignity of his friend and to preserve harmony among his friend's sons. Yet, it turned out that the camel was only useful to help divide the herd and was not really needed. So the friend was left with the camel anyway.

We may have experienced an opportunity to give something away to someone in need, making a sacrifice, only to find that it was either returned to us or circumstances changed and we did not need to give it away. Yet, we were rewarded with the feeling of satisfaction of having sacrificed for others. We feel God's blessings showering down upon us. We thank God that we chose to give rather than to be selfish.

There is no greater joy that can fill our heart than giving. All who have given selflessly may have experienced that one never loses when one gives. We find more and more blessings raining down upon us unasked for, and our hearts are filled with godly love.

God Comes in Many Forms

Every evening, a religious family sat down to dinner and said prayers over the food. The father concluded the prayer by asking that God come to the table as a guest of the family and bless their food. Each night the father closed the prayer with the same words before they could start their dinner. The young son listened attentively to this prayer every night.

One day, the young boy asked his father, "Why do you keep asking God to come every night when God never comes?"

The father had no reply, but managed to say, "Well, son, we will just keep waiting. I am sure that God hears our invitation each night."

The son said, "Well, father, if you really expect God to come for dinner, how is it that you never even set a place for the Lord at the table? If you really want God to come, then we should set a place for the Lord."

The father was embarrassed by the boy's keen observation and questions. To put a stop to his questions, the father set a place at the table for God. He put down fine silverware, a plate, a napkin, and a glass. As soon as he had finished setting the table, there was a knock on their door. The boy was excited thinking that God would now come.

When he opened the door, he found a small young homeless boy standing at the door. He was shivering because it was freezing outside. The son was at first shocked because he expected to see God. But then he thought for a moment and said, "I guess God could not come today so God sent this boy instead in God's place. Come on in." And he sat the boy at God's empty place at the dinner table.

This anecdote is a reminder that we never know in what form God will come to us. Many only want to serve God directly. We do not realize that it is also God's work to serve God's creation. Each day, life presents us with opportunities to help others. When we help others, we are helping God's children. All are a part of God. When we turn away someone, we are turning away one of God's children. How can we expect God to be pleased with us when we do not help one of God's creations?

Saints and Masters are models of selfless service. They sacrifice their lives for others. Time and again they stop what they are doing to tend to the needs of others. They are an active part of their communities, providing help to whoever comes to them.

Spirituality is not running away from helping others. It is being sensitive and attuned to the needs of others. As the great poet-saint Sant Darshan Singh Ji Maharaj has said:

> *We are communing with the moon and the stars,*
> *But have not reached the heart of our neighbor.*

While we try to progress spiritually through our meditation, we should start expanding our hearts to include all creation as one family. We will find that without wanting anything in return for ourselves, we will begin to serve from our own hearts. When we do so, we will find that we truly earn God's pleasure.

Honesty and Truthfulness

Be Honest with Our Selves

One of the divine qualities of the soul is truthfulness. While the soul lives the path of truth, the mind plays the game of deceitfulness and untruth. To progress spiritually, we need to identify with our soul. This entails exercising the virtue of truthfulness.

Mahatma Gandhi is an example of one who practiced the virtue of truth. He valued truthfulness. During one of his periods of nonviolent protest to help win independence for India, he was arrested and put in jail. One of the rules of this particular jail was that prisoners were to receive no newspapers or news of the outside world.

One day, a doctor who was friendly with Gandhi Ji came to visit him in prison. There was some news that he thought Gandhi needed to know about how the movement for nonviolence was doing. Knowing that the prison rules were that prisoners could not get news of the outside world, the doctor, who had brought a newspaper, pulled out some of his papers and placed them on Gandhi's cot in his prison cell. The doctor proceeded to talk to Gandhi about his health and comforts. When it was time for the doctor to leave, he put all the papers from the cot back into his pocket, except he left the newspaper.

When Gandhi saw the newspaper lying there, he refused to read it. In fact, he was so honest he did not want to break prison rules by even looking at it. Instead, Gandhi turned his back away from the newspaper on the bed and faced the corner of his cell the entire night. He sat up the entire night, with his face toward the corner so he would not see the newspaper or touch it.

The following morning, the doctor returned to visit Gandhi. Seeing the newspaper lying on the cot in the same place he had left it the previous night, the doctor said, "I am sorry, but I left the newspaper here by mistake."

A smile crossed Mahatma Gandhi's face and he replied, "Yes, you sentenced me to spend the whole night in a corner!"

Such was Gandhi's honesty that even if no one saw him read the paper, he did not want to be dishonest, because he himself would know he broke his agreement to follow the prison rules while there. How many of us live by such a degree of honesty?

What we do not realize is that we may hide what we do from others, but we cannot hide from God and our own soul. We have to live with the fruits of our actions. The soul has the virtue of honesty. Whenever we are faced with a choice of being honest or dishonest, we can follow the dictates of our soul or those of our mind. The mind leads us into many excuses to be dishonest. It has a thousand reasons why we should lie, cheat, steal, or deceive others. But the soul knows only honesty.

If we want to make spiritual progress, we should identify more and more with our soul. Getting closer to our true state—the soul within us—means beginning to practice honesty in our own dealings. Is it worth delaying our spiritual progress by a small lie or dishonest act? Is the little money we may make by deceiving others or cheating others worth the delay we make in reuniting our soul with the eternal Creator and experiencing the true spiritual riches within? Those riches are eternal and will stay with us permanently.

Truth Always Finds a Way

Those who seek spiritual attainment gain a respect for the quality of truthfulness. In daily life we are faced with the choice of telling the truth or uttering an untruth. Many people feel that no one will ever find out if they tell a lie or deceive others. Thus, to make some gain for themselves or to get away with something, people often tell a lie. Little do we realize that truth always finds a way to reveal itself. Sooner or later, the truth will come out. When we are truthful in all our dealings, we have nothing to fear and nothing to hide. Others come to respect and trust us, and our slate is clean when we try to enter the spiritual kingdom.

A story from the times of Akbar and Birbal illustrates the importance of being truthful in all our dealings. Once there was a religious man who wanted to take a pilgrimage. He did not want to take a chance of losing his life savings, so he went to his friend to ask him to hold them for him while he was on pilgrimage. He asked his friend to join him in the forest so he could secretly tell him of his wishes without anyone knowing it. So the man and his friend went to the forest.

The religious man said, "I am going on pilgrimage but do not know when I will return. Could you be so kind as to hold this bag with my life savings in it safely until my return? I will collect it from you when I get back." The friend agreed to guard his money and took the bag from him. The following day the religious man left on pilgrimage.

Many years passed but the religious man did not return. Then, one morning, the religious man returned as an old man from pilgrimage and knocked on the door of his friend.

"I have returned from my pilgrimage and would like my money back," said the religious man. The friend changed the subject and began to talk about other things. The religious man kept coming back to the subject of his money, but his friend kept changing the subject.

Finally, the old man insisted, "Can I please have my money back?"

The friend said, "I don't know what you are talking about. You never gave me any money."

The old man was shocked and shouted, "I never expected you, my friend, to act this way. Please give me back my money that I entrusted you to watch for me."

The friend said, "Are you crazy? You must be imagining things. You never gave me any money. You are lying."

The man kept requesting his money, but the friend turned him out of his house. In despair, the religious man decided to bring the case before Emperor Akbar. The emperor listened patiently to the old man's story. He then called for Birbal, his wisest advisor, and asked him to take care of the case for him.

Birbal listened to the old man's complaint and then had his friend summoned.

When the friend arrived, Birbal asked him whether the old man had given him any money.

The friend responded, "Sir, he is a big liar. He never gave me anything."

Birbal looked perplexed, and turned to the old man, saying, "You say you gave him a bag containing money. Do you have any witnesses?"

The old man said, "I do not have any witnesses because I gave the bag to the man in the forest, beneath a mango tree."

Birbal said, "You are foolish to say you have no witnesses. You gave it to him under a mango tree. Can't you get help from the mango tree in this matter? Go immediately to that mango tree and tell it that Birbal wants it to appear before him in this case. Go, quickly." The old man was surprised at Birbal's request, but did as he was ordered. He departed for the forest to bring the mango tree as a witness.

In the meantime, Birbal asked the friend to have a seat by his side. An hour passed. When the old man did not come back, Birbal started to pretend to talk to himself out loud. He said, "Why is that old man taking so long? He is taking such a long time to do such a small task!"

The friend responded, "But sir, he can't possibly return so soon. He would not have even reached that place yet."

Birbal asked him, "What do you mean? Do you mean to say that this place is so far away from here that it would take him a long time to get there?"

"Yes," responded the friend. "The place which the old man says that he gave me the money is very far away from here."

"So, I see," said Birbal, who then kept quiet.

After a long time, the old man returned, out of breath. He said to Birbal, "Sir, I gave the message to the tree, but it did not say anything to me."

Birbal said, "Do not worry about it. The tree has already proved to me that this man did receive the bag of money from you."

Birbal then turned to the friend and said, "You have one more chance to admit your guilt and return the money to this man."

But the friend insisted, "But he never gave me any money."

Finally, Birbal said, "If that is so, then how is it you knew that the tree under which he claimed to give you the bag of money was far from here? Are you prepared to admit your guilt now?"

At this point, the friend realized he was caught in his own lie, and he bowed down to Birbal's feet and begged forgiveness. He then returned the money to the old man.

This story illustrates that sooner or later the truth we try to hide will be uncovered. When we tell a lie, we have to tell so many more to cover up the first one. It is hard to keep so many lies straight in our mind. While the truth is one and is easy to remember, a lie weaves a tangled web in which we have to remember all the various strands. It is hard to sleep peacefully at night when we are worried about someone's finding out the truth. It is better to tell the truth and be done with it, and sleep and meditate peacefully, than go through life with the fear of our being found out hanging over our heads.

Spiritual progress depends on a stillness of mind, free of mental entanglements and attachments. Being the keeper of a lie is an unnecessary entanglement that occupies our time and attention and keeps us from the peace of mind needed to go back to God. By thinking twice before telling a lie, we can live a life of peace and tranquility and speed our journey back to God.

Humility

The Strength of Humility

A group of soldiers was trying to lift a large piece of timber. The corporal stood by the side, commanding the men to heave harder to lift the timber. A stranger rode by on his horse and observed the scene.

He said to the corporal, "Don't you think if you helped them, the strength of one more man might help them to lift the timber? Why don't you help them?"

The corporal replied, "That is not my job. I am the corporal. It is for them to do that work. That is not the work of a corporal!"

With that, the stranger dismounted from his horse, joined the ranks of the soldiers and helped them to lift the timber. The added strength of one man was all it took to lift the wood.

Having completed the task, the stranger mounted his horse. Before departing he turned to the corporal and said, "The next time you have a piece of timber you need help lifting, corporal, call for the commander-in-chief."

It was then that the men realized that the stranger was none other than George Washington, the first president of the United States, the commander-in-chief of the army.

This story symbolizes true humility. Many feel that we are so important that we cannot do the chores in our family, the menial work, or even the small, behind-the-scenes work in our offices. We feel ourselves to be high and mighty. Interestingly, we find in the lives of evolved people an incredible humility that draws them to work among the lowly workers.

The next time we think of how important we are, or we get a bloated ego, think of the truly great people who humble themselves to be of service to humanity. None is so great that he or she cannot share in the burden of his or her neighbor. We are never so great that we cannot lend a helping hand to someone in need. After all, we are enlivened by God. It is God who makes our life possible and bestows gifts on us. Without God, we are nothing. It is God who makes us who we are.

If we could be like the commander-in-chief and dismount our horses to help one another, we would find the grace of God ready to pour out blessings to us in abundance.

Love for Animals

Compassion for Animals

There is an inspiring story from the life of the saint Eknath. He lived in Maharashtra. Once he was traveling with a group of his followers from Varanasi on pilgrimage to Rameshwaram, in the south. The belief at that time was that if an offering was made to Lord Shiva in the temple at Rameshwaram one would have good luck. So, Eknath and his followers stopped first at the Ganges River to collect some holy water to bring as an offering for Lord Shiva.

As they headed on foot to Rameshwaram, they passed through a thick jungle. The pathway became narrower and narrower. Somehow

Eknath became separated from his followers who could not keep up with him. He decided to stop and wait for them. He sat under a large tree to shade himself from the hot sun. It was extremely hot outside and the earth had grown dry and parched. As Eknath sat there, he spotted a donkey off in the distance. The donkey was lying on the ground. He approached the animal and found the donkey to be dying of thirst. Eknath could feel the pain of the donkey in his own heart. Eknath searched for water in the immediate area but could not find any. He looked at his jug of Ganges water and thought for a moment. Should he give the water to the donkey or save it for an offering for Lord Shiva at the temple? He put the question to his own soul and to God, and immediately he knew what to do. He took the jug of Ganges water and gave it to the donkey to drink. The donkey was so thirsty that he drank every drop.

As he was giving the donkey the holy water, his followers caught up to him. They saw the donkey drinking the water and started questioning the saint.

"What are you doing? This is the holy water we are taking to Lord Shiva," said one.

Another said, "Now our trip to Rameshwaram is wasted. We will have nothing to offer there."

But the saint smiled and told his followers, "A true human being cannot bear to see another living being dying of thirst. This offering to save the donkey's life is far greater than any other offering and brings the most benefit to the giver."

This story illustrates the high degree of vision of a saint and how a God-realized being feels the pain in the hearts of all other living beings. The closer we get to God and our soul, the more compassionate we become toward the pains of others. Sometimes we try to do good to have some gain for ourselves. Some people give in charity to impress others. Some people try to do service to make a show to impress others.

Sometimes, while doing so, we ignore someone who is really in need. We may walk over someone, step on someone, or trample others in our quest to make a show of doing good. But the real service is in listening to the cries of others and tending to their needs. If in doing service to win points for ourselves we break the heart of another or trample on the other person's rights, we have not truly gained any benefit. It is better to live our lives listening to the souls and hearts of others and being sensitive to other people's feelings and needs. When we soothe someone else's heart or apply balm to the wounds of others, we have truly served the Lord. That is the greatest offering.

Healing the Suffering of Animals

There is an account of a holy man who once had to go on a long journey. In those days, people would carry bundles with them. So he packed a bundle and filled it with enough bread to eat on the trip. He traveled on foot, and when night fell, he stopped at a mosque to rest.

The next morning he set out again on the journey. He walked quickly for about ten miles and then decided to stop for breakfast. He sat down and opened his bundle to take out the bread. When he opened the bundle, he found that the bread was full of ants.

"Oh, this is too bad!" he thought.

Most people at this point would be upset that their food had been destroyed. But something else was bothering the holy man. He said, "This is awful. I have taken these poor ants a long way from their home in the mosque. They must be missing their families, parents, and children greatly."

He felt so bad and had so much compassion for the ants and their welfare, that the holy man walked the ten miles back to the mosque to take the ants back to their home.

We find accounts like this in the lives of the saints and mystics. They have a great depth of compassion within them for the suffering of others, from human beings to the smallest of ants.

The more spiritual we grow, the more attuned we are to the murmurings of our soul. Our soul is full of compassion. The more we identify with the mind, the less compassion we feel. The more we identify with the soul, the more compassion we have.

We can gauge our own lives by the depth of compassion we experience for the suffering of others.

How many of us even consider the tender feelings of the lesser brothers and sisters in God? The vegetarian diet is a compassionate one. If we saw what animals had to go through to be used for food, we would feel compassion and would never want to see them hurt.

Let us work toward a state in which we are kind and loving. Let us make sure our words are sweet. Let us make sure we are tender and compassionate to others. Let us soothe the broken hearts with love, affection, and sweet words.

Teacher's Love

The Power of a Teacher's Love

Once there was a schoolteacher who was celebrating her eightieth birthday. The teacher had spent many years teaching in an inner-city school. Before coming to her, many of the students at her school had been involved in antisocial behaviors. But, as the teacher worked there, people noticed a dramatic change in her students. Many of them grew up to be good citizens. Many went on to become doctors, lawyers, teachers, skilled technicians, and businesspeople. People noticed the difference that this teacher made in many of the lives of her students.

It was no wonder that on her eightieth birthday her former students arrived to pay their respects and offer their gratitude to her for all that she had done for them.

The newspapers heard about this grand birthday party and sent a reporter to cover the story. The reporter who interviewed her asked, "What was the secret to your success as a teacher?"

The teacher replied, "As I look around at the young teachers who graduate today, I find that they are focused on the skills in their profession. When I look back, I realize that when I started teaching, all I had to give was love!"

In this simple statement by this lifelong schoolteacher, one finds the secret to the success of the spiritual Masters of all ages. This schoolteacher in the story had the power to transform lives. She took students who lacked virtues and transformed them into ethical people. This is what the spiritual Masters do. They take suffering humanity, filled with anger, lust, greed, attachment, and ego, and transform them into beings filled with nonviolence, selflessness, purity, humility, truth, and love. How do they do this? It is all done through the power of divine love.

If one is told what to do through a heartless order, few people follow it. But, if we love someone and know that someone loves us, then we listen to and respect that person. It is through the love of a parent that a child learns to talk and walk. It is through the love of a teacher that we learn the academic subjects. It is through love of a mentor that we learn a skill. It is through the divine love of a spiritual Master that we become spiritual ourselves.

We have seen in the lives of great saints how kind they were. They positively transformed the lives of those who met them. Love has the greatest transformative power.

True Teacher

There is a story from the Indian tradition about a king of India who had five sons. Unfortunately, they were not smart and had a hard time learning anything. In fact, the king considered them all to be fools. They did not take their work seriously, clowned around, and did not want to learn a single thing from their studies.

One day, the king sat down with his queen and discussed what they should do with their children. After all, one day one of them would have to succeed him and he did not want to entrust his kingdom to an uneducated son. They had tried many tutors, but none of them could get through to their sons. They did not want to learn anything.

They decided to make an offer to their subjects. They announced that anyone in their kingdom who could educate their sons would be rewarded with half the kingdom. One after the other, teachers, tutors, scholars, and learned people came forward to attempt to educate the five princes. But each one left feeling disappointed, as they could not be successful. The princes refused to learn anything.

The king and queen became more frustrated. Their sons acted like complete fools and none of the training offered by the best in the land seemed to have any effect on them.

One day, a renowned scholar and teacher came to the palace and asked the king's permission to try to teach the boys. The king agreed and the teacher tried some new teaching methods to get through to them. He taught them by telling them interesting stories, which captivated their attention.

The boys enjoyed the stories. Four months passed. They looked forward to their lessons with the teacher. But at the end of the four months, when the teacher tested them, he found not one of them remembered a single story. They would enjoy the stories for the moment, but nothing was sinking in. So the teacher tried another approach. This time, after telling the boys a story, he told them that if they wished to hear another one they had to retell the story to each other as a way to remember it. He warned them that if they could not retell the story, they would not be told any more stories.

The sons started listening more attentively to the stories. But not enough to remember the story.

Finally, the teacher took the princes to a well.

"Look at this pulley made of rope with a stone tied to the end of one side of the pulley and a bucket on the other side. When the stone is thrown in the water it pulls up the bucket," said the teacher. "See how over time the rope has made a deep impression on the stone. Just as the rope made a mark on the stone, I want you to go over each story mentally again and again until you remember each one. The stories should make a mark on your minds."

The princes, wanting to hear more and more stories, did what the teacher told them to do. By repeating each story over in their minds, they eventually were able to learn the stories. With time their attention improved and they could learn whatever the teacher taught them.

The king was delighted with the teacher's results. He offered the teacher half the kingdom. But the teacher refused.

The teacher said, "O great king, I am a teacher. What have I to do with owning and ruling a kingdom? I get my joy from teaching. I am satisfied that I have done my duty." With this, he went on his way.

This attitude of the teacher is similar to those held by the great spiritual teachers who come to this world. Their job is to help the wayward souls learn the lessons of spirituality. They are satisfied if they can educate our soul into the spiritual truths — such as meditation and leading an ethical life. If we look at the lives of Buddha, Christ, Guru Nanak, Prophet Mohammed, Mahavira, Moses, and other great saints, we find that they gave of themselves selflessly.

Finding Happiness

The Treasure That Lies Within

Once there was a farmer who lived in a village. The man was poor. He tried to make his living from farming, but could not earn enough for a nice house, good possessions, or fine clothes. He looked so ragged that some of the people in his neighborhood made fun of him. Yet the man was content with what he had. He was a great lover of God and spent his free time in prayer and meditation to the Lord.

Some of the man's friends advised him to make something of himself instead of wasting his time in prayer to God. The man was happy with his own life, but they kept nagging him so much to do something about his circumstances that a seed of doubt was planted in his mind. He began thinking that maybe he could be happier if he were richer.

One night, the farmer had a dream. He dreamt that a divine being told him to go into the city where he would find a huge treasure. When the farmer awoke, being influenced by his friends to seek wealth, he decided to listen to his dream. He undertook the journey to the city. He had not traveled to the city before and was unfamiliar with its laws. A chief of police found him wandering around and picked him up. He brought him to the police station.

The police chief inquired, "What are you doing wandering away day and night?"

The farmer explained, "I am in search of a treasure. I had a dream and it told me I would find a vast treasure here."

The police chief said, "You are a fool. I have had many dreams about finding a treasure. They are only dreams. I ignore every one of them. They are useless dreams. For example, once I dreamed that I should go to a poor hut in a village outside the city. The hut had a stream passing by it. There was a small farm nearby, but the house was a poor one. I was told in the dream that I would find a huge treasure there. But I never went there because visions are not real."

As the police chief was describing the house, the farmer had a shock. The house being described sounded exactly like his own!

The chief of police sent him back to his village. The man was overjoyed at the possibility that the treasure he was seeking might just be in his own front yard.

The farmer went to the spot described by the police chief. He began digging. Sure enough, he uncovered a large treasure chest filled with enough wealth to make him a rich man. He was amazed that all this time there was a hidden treasure right by his own home.

This story describes our condition. We are searching for happiness and love all over the world. Little do we realize that true wealth, true happiness, and true love are waiting within us.

We think that happiness is outside ourselves. We think it lies in wealth, name and fame, possessions, and relationships. But true happiness lies within. God lies within us. God's love is within. There is nothing in the outer world that can compare to that. Instead of seeking the true treasure outside ourselves, we should sit in meditation and find the true wealth within. Then we will find our lives filled with love, bliss, and eternal peace and happiness.

Impermanence of Life

Prepare Our Soul for Eternity

Once there was a man who was in the later stages of life. He began thinking about the end of his life and that he might die one day. He thought of how graveyards are filled with tombstones and how flowers are placed there for the dead which the dead never see.

He decided, "I want to know where I will be buried, in what casket I will be buried, and what kind of flowers will be put on my graveyard before I die. After I am dead, I will never see them." So the man spent the last two years of his life preparing his own burial place. He went to the cemetery and picked out the plot in which he would be buried, happy to see it before he died. He went to the funeral parlor and selected a casket in which he would be buried.

He thought, "This is the home I will have after I am dead. I am glad to see it before I die." He went to the flower shop and selected the flowers he wanted placed over his grave. He was proud that he could see the flowers, whereas all the dead and buried people never see them. Then he called a meeting of his family and friends and distributed many of his personal belongings. Finally, he handed his son his will. At that moment, the man collapsed and died.

The man had spent the last two years of his life preparing his body for his physical death, but had not done anything to prepare his soul.

Many of us are no different from this man. He spent his last two years taking care of where his body would be kept after he died. But he did not pay any attention to preparing his soul for eternal life. If we look at our lives, many of us are concerned only with our body. We are worried about how to feed it, clothe it, and shelter it. Although we must work to earn money, we focus more on working for the care of our physical body than on our soul. Besides being concerned about our food, clothing, and shelter, we put in more time than needed to shop and decorate our homes or our bodies. If we analyze the time we spend on our physical selves and then analyze the time we spend on our soul, we might find a large discrepancy.

If we wish to make the best use of the remaining years of our life, we could put more attention into our soul. Preparing our soul for the life Beyond means spending time in meditation and selfless service. It means trying to be a good person and helping people whenever we can. It means spending time analyzing and improving our character. It means keeping remembrance of the Lord. What matters in the Beyond is whether we were a loving person.

In our daily lives, set priorities. Let us not neglect our soul due to overemphasis on the physical body. Find some balance in our lives. While we need to take care of our body and those of our family, make sure we spend sufficient time in caring for our soul. After all, when the final hour comes, our body will turn to dust, but our soul will live on. Spend time empowering our soul for now and the Beyond.

God's Omnipresence, Protection, and Mercy

God's Mercy

There is a legend that when God wanted to create human beings, God called all the angels together to get their advice. As God sat on a heavenly throne, the angels stood around and, one by one, God asked each his or her opinion.

The Angel of Justice said, "Do not create humans. If you do, they will commit all kinds of evil against each other. They will be cruel, mean, and violent, and do unjust acts."

Next, the Angel of Truth said, "Do not create humans. They will lie and deceive, and cheat and steal from each other. In fact, they will even deceive and lie to You, O Lord."

The Angel of Holiness said, "Do not create humans, O Lord. They will commit many impure acts and bring dishonor to You."

Finally, God turned toward the Angel of Mercy, and asked, "What do you think?"

The Angel of Mercy replied, "Go ahead and create humans, O Lord, for whenever they commit sins and turn away from the spiritual path of truth, righteousness, and holiness, I will take them in my arms, speak loving words to them, and bring them back to You, O Lord."

This story shows the role of the saints, prophets, spiritual Masters, and enlightened beings in our lives. It is true that as human beings we are prone to human weaknesses. We are beset by numerous temptations and attractions that pull us away from our divine nature. But rather than not create humans because they might fail, God created humans to face challenges and learn lessons to overcome obstacles and return to God. God created the saints and Masters to have compassion, mercy, and love for us and guide us to return to our divine nature.

If we do fail, saints and mystics are there to encourage us to try again and not give up. They do not want us to wallow in our guilt and worry about it, but make a firm resolve to do better the next day. Their loving arms are always waiting to embrace us, just as a mother is eager to embrace her child who has fallen in the mud. She cleans him, tells him to avoid the mud, and sends him out again with a kiss on his head. Saints and Masters are all-loving, and no matter what we do, they are always there to take us back in their arms, help us improve, and let us try again.

Like the Angel of Mercy, saints are all compassion. It is their job to take us back to the spiritual path that God has laid out for us. We can make their job easier by remembering their mercy and trying to do better each day. Slowly, day by day, we will find that with their grace and blessings, we will avoid ethical failures so that we can become the divine beings that God intended us to be.

We Cannot Hide from the Lord

Leonardo da Vinci, the famous artist, was at work on his painting *The Last Supper*, in which he showed Christ sitting with his disciples for what was to be his last dinner with them. While painting, Leonardo da Vinci became angry at a particular man. Leonardo lost his temper and began speaking hot words to the man. He even threatened him.

When the man had left, Leonardo returned to his painting. He tried to work on painting Jesus's face, but could no longer do so. He was so upset with himself for becoming angry that he could not calm himself down to continue painting. He tried to go back to work but could not.

Finally, he realized what was wrong. The face of Jesus reminded him of God. Suddenly, Jesus's face became like a pure mirror reflecting back to Leonardo the blemish on his own face. He realized he had committed a wrong in hurting the other man. Unable to face Jesus and God, he put his paints down and sought out the man. Leonardo apologized profusely to him for his bitter words. The man accepted Leonardo's apology.

Leonardo, now at peace, was able to return to his work and finish painting the face of Jesus.

We may think we can hide our thoughts, words, and deeds from God, but we cannot. We may think that God does not know what we do.

The next time we get angry at someone, hurt someone's feelings with our words, hurt someone, or injure any living thing, we should realize that God is watching us. We should reflect upon how we feel after committing such acts. If we sit in stillness, we will realize that we do not feel right after doing a harmful act. We will perceive the voice of conscience reminding us to be good and do good. Once we are in tune with that inner voice, once we listen to the soul, we will find that we will make choices that lead us on the path of goodness. In this way, we will soon find our spiritual journey will be accelerated.

God Is Always With Us

In the early 1900's, Sir Ernest Shackleton dreamed of crossing Antarctica by dogsled. Crossing Antarctica involved a twenty-one-hundred-mile journey. Somehow, humanity dreams of taking challenges that no one has ever taken before. If someone conquers a challenge, then others either want to replicate it or break the record. It is part of the human spirit. So his twenty-eight-member crew decided to take up the challenge. Unfortunately, three days after setting sail, the ship taking them to Antarctica became frozen in an ice pack. Trapped, the men had to wait ten months for spring to melt the ice and free the ship. Shackleton kept morale high as they stayed alive with the provisions they brought. When spring came, the ice melted, but disaster struck when the ship was crushed by the ice. They could not make it on foot across the ice to the open sea, so they camped for five months on an ice floe, eating rationed food. When they felt the ice floe break up, they knew they could travel by water moving from one ice floe to another. Shackleton led the men with their three life boats and provisions to sail through and across ice floes one-hundred-eighty miles to Elephant Island. They braved snow, hail, sleet, and rain as they huddled their soaked bodies together in the boats to stay warm.

On the deserted Elephant Island, Shackleton realized they would die unless he went for help. He left most of his crew there with provisions, knowing he had to reach the whaling station on Georgia Island. He and five others took the largest lifeboat, twenty-two feet long, and crossed the most treacherous sea of Antarctica to reach the closest, inhabited station. Gale-winds, hurricanes, and towering waves threatened their lives. They were frost-bitten, tortured by thirst, and wet, but after seventeen days finally reached Georgia Island. Their lifeboat was too damaged to go further, and they were on the wrong side of the island. To reach the station, they had to cross an icy mountain range. Shackleton took two of the men with him. They used nails from the lifeboat on the bottom of their thinning boot soles for traction, brought two compasses, some ropes, and provisions and set out on the thirty-mile journey across icy mountains and glaciers. Thirty-six hours later, scrawny and hardened by their ordeal, Shackleton and his two crew members reached the whaling station, their first contact with civilization in seventeen months. Shackleton returned in a rescue boat for the rest of his crew, and when he got back to Elephant Island found that not a single man had perished.

When Shackleton was asked how they made it through such difficulties, he told his friends that he felt the presence of an unseen Power guiding them on this journey.

How can a human survive that? In truth, we do not survive these things on our own. We are too frail and too helpless against the power of nature. It is the God Power within us that gives us the strength, the power, and the courage to face our challenges.

Each at one time or another has had to face a physical challenge. Sometimes we wondered if we would make it through. Yet when we did survive, we marvelled at how we did it. Each of these experiences is a proof of a higher Power that is always with us. We are never alone. God is always with us.

Whenever we have to face a challenge that we feel is too difficult, we should keep in mind that we do not have to face it alone. The unseen Hand of God is always with us. We may not see God. But God is definitely there. At times, we too feel a presence with us. The more receptive we are, the more we can feel that presence. Whether we see it or not, it is there.

So whenever we look at the challenges we have to face, we should remember those who had even greater struggles, and they made it through. God is always there, guiding our life. Whatever happens to us is in God's Hands.

Face life's challenges fearlessly. Do our best, but leave the outcome in God's will. God is always with us, guiding us through the rough waters of life.

God Can Be Seen in the Microcosm

There is a parable about a man who went to the barbershop. After the barber cut his hair, he held a mirror in front of the man's face to show him his new haircut. As the barber held the mirror, the man could see in it that the king was passing behind him with his long entourage.

The barber excitedly said to the man, "Turn around and see the king passing."

The man replied calmly, "There is no need for me to turn around, for I have seen the king passing in the mirror."

It is said that the great Biblical prophet Ezekiel was standing on the banks of a river. While gazing into the water, he passed into a meditative state. Suddenly as he looked into the river water, he had a glimpse of the seven Heavens and the celestial angels, and the glory of God was revealed to him. All this was revealed to him while gazing into the water.

These two examples together illustrate a profound point. God can be seen in the microcosm of the soul. Many think God is a power that exists outside of us. People try to look for God above us or around us. Yet, God is found within us. The entire macrocosm of God is contained in the microcosm of our soul.

The man having his hair cut saw the reflection of the king in the mirror. The great mystic saw the vision of Heaven while looking into the river. Similarly, we can see God by looking into the reflecting mirror of our soul. Meditation is just that. It is a practice of looking into our true self to find the Overself. It is a process of identifying our soul to identify with God.

When we look into our soul, we are looking to find God there. That is why purity of soul is so important. The reason we cannot always see God in our soul is that our soul has been mired in layers and layers of dirt and grime. This dirt has accumulated over our soul through ages and ages of actions and reactions. We have been engaged in many thoughts, words, and deeds that were negative. We not only covered ourselves with the grime of our own actions, but we also have weights that we incurred due to the reactions of our thoughts, words, and deeds. These layers have sullied the crystal-clear mirror of our soul and we cannot clearly see God there. These layers have muddied the river water so that the heavenly visions cannot be reflected.

Finding the macrocosm in the microcosm requires cleaning the mirror of our heart. We need not look far to find God, but we must look through layers that we have accumulated.

We can clean these layers by not incurring any new ones. We can burn off our old layers by sitting in meditation. Then, bit by bit, the mirror can become clean. We can find the shining Light of God reflected there. We will find that our soul is a part of the same Light of God. We will find that God is within us all the time, waiting to be uncovered.

Just as there was no difference between the barber seeing the king in the mirror or seeing the king in real life, similarly, there is no difference between the God that is omnipotent and the God that resides in our soul. God is God and is the same whether appearing in you or me, in one person or the next. It is one and the same.

We can clean our heart through ethical living, selfless service, and meditation. Then we will be able to look into the mirror of our heart and find the Lord there.

God Supports Good and Bad Alike

The great mystic Sufi saint Rabia Basri had unflinching faith in God throughout her life. She lived a simple life. Her friends were often concerned about whether she had enough on which to survive. They often came to visit her and offer her assistance. Whenever they did so, she gave them this reply: "I feel ashamed to ask for worldly things even from the one who made the world and to whom all the world belongs; therefore, how can I ask help from those to whom the world does not belong?"

Her friends left feeling frustrated that she placed so much reliance upon God that she continually refused help from them.

On another occasion, her saintly friend Hasan of Basra came to visit her. When he arrived he found a wealthy man outside of her hut waiting to go in. He was carrying a bag of gold, which he was hoping to offer her. As Hasan came near, he found the wealthy man was weeping.

"Why do you weep?" Hasan asked him.

The man replied, "I am shedding tears because I am so moved by Rabia. She is a great saint of our times. If it were not for her blessings, humanity would perish. I wish to give her this offering for her service, but I fear she won't accept it. If you plead for me that she should take it, she may listen to you and accept it."

So Hasan entered Rabia's hut and delivered the message from the wealthy man.

Rabia gave Hasan a side glance and refused the wealthy man's offering of gold, with this reply: "Shall God who provides for those who slander and speak against God not provide for those who love God? God does not refuse to provide food and sustenance to those who speak unworthily of God; how then can God refuse sustenance to one whose soul is overflowing with love for God?"

This example from Rabia's life makes us think about our own trust in God. We often worry about whether there will be enough money each month to pay the bills. We wonder if we can sustain our home mortgage or rent. We are concerned about the medical bills of our family. We see the cost of food rising and we wonder how we can keep making enough to afford the basic necessities of life. In times when the stock market takes a dip we worry about our financial future. What we fail to realize is the truth that Rabia herself came to realize. God provides for all the souls who come into this world, whether they are those who live a good life or those who are filled with sins and commit negative acts.

Billions of people are born into the world. Some people live a godly, virtuous life. Some people commit crimes and do evil acts. Yet, God lets the sun shine on each of them alike. God sends rain to fall on the good and bad alike. God provides food on this planet for the good and bad alike. If God takes care of those who slander God or commit ungodly acts, why shouldn't God take care of those who are good people who love God?

When we look at life through the eyes of the soul, we trust that God will take care of us. When we see the world through a godly vision, we find that God is loving us and supporting each of us, whether we are saints or sinners. God does not discriminate between the different types of people. All are God's children and God supports good and bad alike.

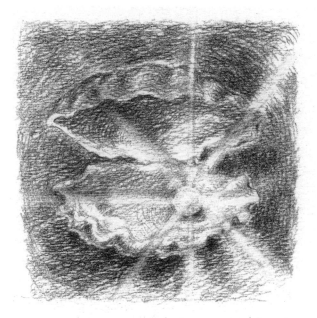

Love of God

A Gift for the Lord

One day, an elderly woman visited the great American president, Abraham Lincoln. The woman had requested an audience with the president and was given an appointment. When she arrived, she carried with her a covered basket.

The president greeted her and, expecting her to be bringing him another problem, asked, "My good woman, what is in the basket?"

She uncovered the basket and said, "Dear Mr. President, I have brought you some fresh-baked cookies."

The president looked at her and said, "And is there anything else?"

She said, "No, sir, I have come here today not to ask any favor for myself or for anyone. I heard that you liked cookies and I came here to bring you this basket."

Tears came to his eyes and he stood speechless.

Finally, he said, "Your thoughtful and unselfish deed greatly moves me. Thousands of people have come to my office since I became president, but you are the first one to come asking no favor for yourself or for somebody else!"

This historical account can easily describe our relationship with God and the saints and Masters. If we were to sit in God's place, we would find most people come to God when they want a favor for themselves or for somebody else. People usually pray to God when they are in trouble and need help. People usually come to God when they have physical problems such as sickness or an accident, financial problems, relationship problems, difficulties with their grades in school, or problems in their career. Few people sit in remembrance of God to show their appreciation and love for God without asking for a favor for themselves.

The best gift we can give to the Lord is to come to God out of love for God. What we do not realize is that God is like a loving parent. We should ask God for nothing but God. Then we will find that we will receive far more than if we had come to God for a favor.

God wants to bestow all blessings on us. But we come to God asking for small things. When God grants our wish to solve one problem, we are still left with many other problems. By the following week, that problem is forgotten and a new one arises.

If we were to come to God with a basket of love, we would receive God's grace in abundance. Being filled with God's love, bliss, and joy would help us through many problems. Knowing that God is with us gives us courage and fortitude to face life's difficulties.

Gaining Spiritual Knowledge

The Value of Experience

A professor of English grammar once got into a boat with a boatman. Proud of his accomplishments in the literary field, he asked the boatman, "Have you ever studied the science of grammar?"

The boatman said, "No, I haven't."

With sarcasm, the grammar professor replied, "Then you have wasted half your life!"

The boatman was upset by the professor's rudeness, but he remained cool outwardly.

Soon, a storm moved in as they sailed across the water. Suddenly, the boat became caught in a vortex of water and they could not maneuver the boat out of it. Fearing that the boat would capsize, the boatman yelled over the roaring waves, "O professor, do you know how to swim?"

The grammar professor replied with contempt, "Certainly not. Don't expect me to know swimming. I never wasted my time with such a pastime."

The boatman told him, "Then, since the boat is going to sink in this tidal wave of a whirlpool, it is *you* who have wasted the other half of your life by not learning how to swim, because you are about to drown!"

This story told by Maulana Rumi in his *Masnavi* points to an important truth. It asks us to contemplate how we spend our lives and what we value. The professor was filled with pride and ego about his intellectual knowledge, but it did not help him when it came to the practical experience of swimming. His life depended upon his ability to swim, but he did not value that activity during his life. He was busy studying grammar books and did not feel he would ever be in the position to need to learn anything else.

Most of us are in the same boat. We spend our lives pursuing physical and intellectual goals, but we remain ignorant of spirituality. When the tidal wave of physical death is upon us, we have no spiritual skills to help us through the end of our life. When we get the news that we have a terminal illness, or suddenly we are faced with our mortality, we panic. We do not know what to do. We have not spent our lives learning about the true meaning of life and death, and we fear our end.

Those who have spent their life learning to swim in the spiritual stream through meditation have nothing to fear. They face their end with calm and fearlessness. Why? They have already seen the splendors of the afterlife while in this life. They have learned the art of rising above body-consciousness and have witnessed firsthand the realms Beyond. What have they to fear when their physical end comes? They know how to swim into the Beyond when the physical boat of their body is about to capsize.

Too many people ignore the reality of physical death until it is too late. They feel that intellectual knowledge and amassing physical wealth, name, and power are more important. But when death nears, they realize their intellectual knowledge and their worldly possessions are of little use. At this point, they regret that they have not spent more time learning about their soul, about God, and the realms Beyond.

Those who learn about spirituality early in life are fortunate. They can devote some time daily to their spiritual practices so they can master the art of rising above body-consciousness in this very life. Like swimming, it takes practice. Daily meditation will build up our spiritual abilities so that we can reach a point at which we can experience the spiritual realms within.

If we can master the art of meditation, then, like the boatman who knew how to swim, we can successfully cross the turbulent ocean of life and find safety in the spiritual harbor.

Choose Your Company Wisely

In some places, people plant a poorer quality rose next to a higher quality rose. This is done to prevent the poorer quality rose from self-pollination, which would genetically continue the poorer quality rose. The concept is designed so that the higher quality rose will pollinate and raise the poorer quality rose to a higher standard.

This principle can guide us in our own lives as well. It is said that a person is known by the company he or she keeps. If we want to be a wealthy person, we should keep the company of rich people. In this way, we would start to think and act like them, and we too might become rich. If we wish to become an athlete, we should spend time with athletes. Thus, we would be motivated to live like they do. We would find ourselves exercising more, keeping fit, watching our diet, and practicing our sport. If we wish to be a writer, we should stay with writers and become inspired to follow that craft.

Similarly, if we wish to develop spiritually, we should keep the company of people who have developed themselves spiritually. Amid such people, we would spend more time engaged in thinking about God and the soul, talking about matters spiritual, and spending time in spiritual practices. If we spent time with someone who meditates, we would be more likely to meditate. If we kept the company of those who value ethical living and practice noble virtues, we would find ourselves acting the same way.

Evaluate the company we keep. Do we find ourselves choosing friends who lead us into the pursuit of poor choices for our personal growth, or do we find ourselves choosing friends who will help us lead a spiritual life? When we wish to be warm, we sit by fire. When we wish to be cool, we sit near an air-conditioner or a block of ice. When we wish to lead a spiritual life, we can find people who are spiritually minded and spend time in their company.

If we are fortunate enough to be in the company of one who is spiritually realized, then that company is even better. Such a person radiates the breath of spirituality that can breathe spiritual awareness into us. Being in the environment of such a person will help focus our attention on the spiritual values of life. That very atmosphere speaks directly to our soul. Our soul is magnetized to one who has realized the soul. This pull uplifts us and focuses our attention on the spiritual gifts within ourselves.

If we wish to improve in our meditations, think about how we spend time during the day. If we spent time in the company of a spiritually realized being and spiritually minded people, we would find that our attention would be more concentrated and our meditations would be more fruitful. Choosing our company wisely can help us progress further on the spiritual way.

Lessons of the Mind and of the Soul

When we start out on a spiritual path, there are two elements involved in learning the spiritual teachings. One is the theoretical side in which we satisfy our mind's questions, and the other is the practical side in which we experience the spiritual truths for ourselves in the depths of our soul. While it is important to be well versed in both aspects, there comes a point in which we must focus our attention on doing the actual practice of meditation to gain true experience. Overemphasis on the theoretical side can take our attention too far away from the practices we need to perform. While we must satisfy the mind and have our questions answered, we do not want to get into mental wrangling, for that is like a spider web from which we may have difficulty escaping.

To illustrate this point, look at the wisdom of the great Lord Buddha. Buddha spent forty-five years selflessly teaching the spiritual truths. He wanted to help suffering souls gain enlightenment and escape the karmic wheel of life that binds them to this world. Buddha was full of compassion and served humanity without any concern for his own comfort. He sacrificed himself so that others could find the road to Nirvana. It is said Buddha toured for eight months out of each year to teach people the way to salvation. The only time he did not tour was during the rainy season, in which he stayed in one place. He gave out his teachings to everyone, irrespective of their caste, religion, color, or social status. He gave all an equal chance to find the way to enlightenment.

One day, a disciple by the name of Malunkyaputta wanted an interview with Lord Buddha. Malunkyaputta had a restless mind, and during his meditations he was always pondering questions such as, "Is the world infinite or finite? Or is the soul identical with the human body?" Instead of meditating and stilling the mind, he ended up spending his meditation time thinking over these philosophical questions. So, during his interview with Buddha, the disciple told Buddha of the difficulties he had in his meditations.

The disciple said, "O Blessed One, please answer these questions. If you do, I will remain on the spiritual path. If you do not answer these questions, I will leave your Holy Order."

Buddha replied, "O Malunkyaputta, did I ever ask you to take up this path and did I promise you that I would answer these intellectual wranglings?"

The disciple sheepishly replied, "No."

Buddha lovingly explained, "Whoever worries about these meaningless speculations such as whether the world is infinite or finite, or whether the soul looks like the body, is taking away time from the spiritual practices. It is just like someone who is shot by an arrow who instead of letting the doctor treat him to get out the poison starts saying, 'I will not allow my wound to be treated until I know who is the man who shot me, what kind of person is he, is he tall or short, what type of bow and arrow did he use, or what color is his skin.' The key is to get treatment first. Similarly, if we say we will not do our spiritual practices until we get answers to these mental questions about whether the universe is eternal or not, and other such questions, then one may pass one's whole life and never reach the spiritual goal."

Buddha further explained, "I teach what is important to know and not what is unimportant. I want to help people solve the problems of sorrow and suffering in this life. What is useful is how to lead the spiritual life leading to enlightenment."

To further illustrate this point, one day, while in the Simsapa forest near Kosambi, Buddha was sitting with his disciples.

Buddha picked up a few leaves and asked his disciples, "What is your opinion? Which is more? Is it the few leaves in my hand, or the leaves in the forest around us?"

The disciples said, "O blessed one, you have very few leaves in your hand, while there are many more in the forest."

Buddha then told them, "It is the same with my teachings. Of everything I know, I have only told you a little. What I have not told you is much more, like the leaves in the forest. Why did I not tell you everything I know? The reason is that all that information is not useful. That information that will not lead to enlightenment, I have not told you. I have only told you that which you need to know to gain the spiritual experience and find salvation."

As we think about our own lives, many get involved in intellectual wrangling. But there comes a point when we find that the mind will never stop its wrangling. We have to discriminate which questions will help our spiritual progress and which ones are merely to satisfy the intellect's curiosity. There are thousands of pages written in all religions on the theoretical side of mysticism. If we were to start reading all those pages now, we might never finish them all in our short life span. People who are steeped in the theoretical side of religion can spend years debating each point found in the scriptural writings and never find any solution. In this short time that we have, it is far better to spend time in our spiritual practices so that we can rise above our limited intellect and come in contact with our soul. Then, we will not have to wonder about the answers, for we will know them for certain and see them for ourselves. Our soul has all the answers, because our soul is one with the Lord.

Let us not waste our precious meditation time thinking over the intricacies of the universe. Instead, we can use that time to keep the mind still so that the soul can come in contact with the inner Light. By absorption in that Light, the soul will awaken to the truths lying within. It will be open to receive the hidden wisdom within us. Then, there will be no more need for questions, for we will experience for ourselves the truths within.

If we feel there is some point blocking our inward journey or disturbing our mind so much so that we cannot meditate, and in all sincerity we need a solution, we need to get it resolved. But if we are merely trying to satisfy our curiosity as a sport or hobby, we are wasting time that could be better used by tapping within ourselves and getting answers from the soul.

As we sit in meditation, seek the inner wisdom. Let us sit in perfect stillness, with the mind calm and quiet. We will find that we will not only receive spiritual enlightenment to satisfy our soul, but as a by-product we will come to know all there is to know to satisfy our mind as well.

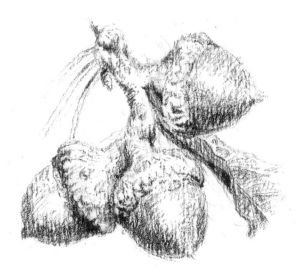

Spiritual Practice

The Best Soil for the Soul

Deep within us is our soul, full of Light, love, and peace. However, layers of mind, matter, and illusion hide our soul. While the soul wants to enjoy its state of love and bliss, it is held back by the mind's incessant need to satisfy its desires. The mind gets enjoyment from the pleasures of the world. Unfortunately, those attractions are temporary. Because they can be taken from us, destroyed, or lost, our mind also goes through an incredible amount of pain and suffering. Thus, our life is a merry-go-round in which we experience the cycle of pain and pleasure.

If we could identify with our soul, we would be in continual happiness and peace. Enlightened beings who have realized their soul wish that others experience the same grandeur within themselves. Out of love for humanity and a desire to end human suffering, they try to teach others how to find their soul.

Buddha was one of the world's greatest spiritual teachers. He brought to the world a way for people to reach enlightenment. He was posed a question that gives us guidance on how we can take advantage of the wisdom of the saints and mystics.

One day, the head of a village approached Lord Buddha. The village head asked, "Is a Buddha compassionate to all living creatures?"

Buddha replied, "Yes."

The headmaster continued, "Does the Buddha give out his teachings in full to some people and not to others?"

To reply to this, the Buddha related a parable, saying, "Let us compare this to the situation of a farmer. Let us suppose that the farmer had three different fields of soil. The soil in one field was excellent. It was highly fertile and rich. The second field had mediocre soil. The third field had poor soil in which not much could grow. Let us also suppose the farmer wanted to sow his seeds. In which field do you think he would plant them?"

The village head replied, "He would first plant them in the field with the excellent soil. After filling that field with seeds, he would move on to plant the rest of the seeds in the mediocre soil. He might or might not plant at all in the field with poor soil. Rather than waste that seed, he might use it to feed the animals."

The Buddha explained, "It is the same with the spiritual teachings. The disciples who wish to become monks who are seeking truth are like the excellent field. These people receive the full extent of the teachings. They learn the full practice and the way to enlightenment in its entirety. The disciples come to me for Light, for refuge, and for shelter. So I give them the entire teachings because that is what they want."

The Buddha contained, "The lay people are like the mediocre field. They are also disciples, but they do not want to commit their whole lives to the teachings as do the monks. To the lay people, though, I also give the spiritual teachings in the entirety. They too come to me for Light, for refuge, and for shelter."

The Buddha then said, "People who do not wish to follow the spiritual teachings are like the poor soil. They are involved with other pursuits in life. Yet, to these people I also give out the spiritual teachings in their entirety."

At this, the village head was shocked and said, "Why do you give your teachings out to even those who are not ready to listen? Is that not a waste?"

To this, the Buddha replied, "If one day they grasp even one sentence of the teaching and take it to heart, that will give them happiness and blessings for a long time."

Thus, the village head understood that the Buddha had come to give his teachings to the whole world, whether or not all were ready for it, because one day they would be.

We too can learn much from this anecdote. Do we wish to be like the excellent soil, the mediocre soil, or the poor soil? Our soul is crying out for us to prepare the soil for its growth. The soul wishes that we become like the excellent soil so it can grow to be a fruit tree, giving shade and fruit to all. The soul is yearning for us to recognize it. The soul is yearning for the mind to be stilled so it can experience its own full power and glory. It lies in wait for us to prepare the soil. It is pained when our soil is so poor that the seeds of wisdom scattered by the wise saints cannot take hold in it.

The loving and compassionate saints and mystics are spraying seeds of truth, Light, and love all around us. Is the soil in our field ready for it? Or will the seeds be wasted?

We can prepare the soil so that the entire teachings can be sown in us and we can achieve enlightenment. The soil can be prepared by practicing daily meditation in which our mind is still and receptive to the inner Light. We can lead a life of calm and contentment, free of desires that make us stray from the path of ethical values. Desires lead to anger, lust, greed, attachment, and ego. These five thieves disturb our inner peace and are an impediment in the way of our meditations. They keep the mind always agitated and restless. By reducing our desires, we increase the fertility of the field to receive the spiritual gifts within. By living a life of love and service, we purify the field of weeds and make our field ready for life-giving fruit trees which all can enjoy.

As we sit in meditation, cultivate a field that is excellent. Prepare the soil so the soul can blossom. The best soil for the soul is one filled with love, humility, truthfulness, purity, and selflessness and is cultivated with the practice of meditation on the inner Light. In such a soil, the full extent of the wisdom of the saints can bear fruit and we too can receive enlightenment.

Spiritual Light

Bringing Light into Darkness

In life, we are faced with numerous challenges. We may have illnesses, financial or relationship problems, or loss of our reputation. We may face dark spells, but we do not have to be blinded by the darkness. The following story has an instructive message to help us through the dark patches of our life.

There was once a cave that lived underground, as most caves do. Since it spent its entire life in darkness, it had never seen any light.

One day, a voice talked to the cave, and said, "Come up into the light. Come and enjoy the sunlight."

The cave replied, "I do not know what you mean by light. All I have ever known is darkness."

"Come and see for yourself," said the voice.

The cave mustered up enough courage and climbed slowly up from the depths of the earth. Suddenly, it reached the top of the earth and was surrounded by magnificent light, the likes of which the cave had never seen in its life.

"This is beautiful," said the cave.

After enjoying the light for a while, the cave said to the sunlight, "Now it is your turn to come with me and see the darkness."

"What is darkness?" asked the sunlight.

The cave answered, "Come and see for yourself."

One day, the sunlight decided to visit the cave's home. As the sunlight entered the cave, it said, "Now show me your darkness." But with the sunlight there, there was no darkness to be found.

What this story illustrates is the power of light. Wherever there is light, there can be no darkness. Whenever we feel we are in a dark spell of our life, we need only tap into the Light of our soul. We are Light. Our soul is Light. Our true nature is Light. If we would only identify with our true nature, we would find there is no darkness. If we would also bring our own innate goodness and Light into our daily life, we would never be overcome by the darkness of life again.

We each have within us the Light of the soul, which has been described by saints as being equal to the light of sixteen outer suns. But we are not aware of it because we identify ourselves with the outer world of darkness and illusion. If we would invert our attention within through meditation, we would discover that we are Light. Then, whenever the dark spells of life threaten to bring us down, we could invert, find the Light within, and bring it forth into the darkness to dispel it.

Whenever we find we are faced with sickness, financial problems, ignominy, or loss, we can remember that these are but passing clouds in the brilliant sunlit sky. Our true reality is Light and love. When we associate with the temporary illusions of this world, we feel pain. But when we realize that the outer events are but a dream existence, a passing show that is but temporary, we can rise above the pain and disappointment.

When we find sadness in life, let us maintain our inner harmony. When we find misfortune, let us count the numerous times we have experienced good fortune. When we fail, take that as an opportunity to learn from our mistakes and try again. When we find ourselves in darkness, let us close our eyes and focus within until we see the Light. That Light will bring with it peace, joy, and love. It will comfort us and give us strength to carry on. That Light is the Light of God. If we bring that Light into our life, then we too, like the cave in the story, will find that there is no more darkness.

If we sit in meditation, we can experience the Light waiting for us within. Let us not be distracted by the darkness of thought, but instead sit in stillness and wait lovingly for God to shine the Light upon us.

See for Yourself

Theory vs. Practice

Once the great writer Mark Twain was having a discussion with a businessman who was known for being aggressive and ruthless in his dealings with others.

The businessman said to the writer, "Before I die I would like to make a pilgrimage to the Holy Land and climb to the top of Mount Sinai to read the Ten Commandments aloud at the top."

Mark Twain quickly replied, "I have a better idea. Rather than go to Mount Sinai where Moses was given the Ten Commandments, why don't you just stay home here in Boston and practice the Ten Commandments in your life!"

This humorous comment carries a significant meaning. Many of us read the Commandments or advice given by the great saints in the scriptures. Many of us are happy even to preach what our holy books say. But how many of us live up to the teachings we follow?

There is a big difference between knowing the theory and practicing it. It is not enough to read the books or scriptures and know the theory. We need to live up to them in our own lives. If we learn a method of meditation and instructions for progress, that is not enough; we have to actually practice it.

The true heart of the spiritual teachings is in the practice. It is not enough to know what others have said about it. It is essential that we have our own firsthand experience of spirituality. That can be accomplished when we sit in meditation.

Progress is a matter of accuracy. We can become accurate only by practice. Practice makes perfect. If we expect to sit in meditation once or twice in our life and accomplish spiritual progress, we are being unrealistic. We need to practice daily.

It is said that if we take one step toward God, God will take a hundred steps toward us. The time we spend in meditation will be richly rewarded.

Instead of merely reading the Ten Commandments, live them. If we do our meditations and lead ethical lives, observing the virtues of nonviolence, truthfulness, purity, humility, selfless service, and love for all, we will be blessed with inner vision. We will have the proof for ourselves of the existence of our soul and God.

Mind and Soul

The Strongest Enemy

During the time of Guru Gobind Singh, there was a great rishi who gave up everything to go to a forest to meditate. There was also a king who had already conquered many other territories and their people. One day, the king set his ambition on conquering the rishi to make him obey his commands. People thought it was strange that the king would focus on conquering a rishi who had no property, kingdom, or wealth. But it turned out that the rishi had previously been a king before giving up his kingdom for the spiritual life. This made the present king have an obsession with wanting to conquer the rishi. So the king gathered his entire army to prepare for battle.

The army marched into the deep forest. The army finally reached the rishi, who was sitting in the woods, deep in meditation.

The king waited for the rishi to come out of meditation, but he kept on sitting there. Finally, the king became restless and shook the rishi out of meditation.

The king shouted, "Prepare for a fight. I have come to do battle with you."

The rishi surveyed the scene calmly. He saw the great army and said, "Fight! I ran away from my worldly life for fear of my one great enemy. I came here to hide in the woods from this enemy. My soul shudders in fear when I hear the sound of my enemy's name. Just to think of this enemy's name causes my heart to quiver."

The king listened carefully as the rishi continued to describe his feared enemy. Finally, the king became angry and shouted, "Is your enemy stronger than me?"

The rishi replied, "Even the thought of this enemy destroys my soul. I left everything to escape from this enemy."

The king said, "Tell me the name of this enemy of yours."

The rishi said, "There is no use in telling you who it is. You will never be able to conquer him."

The king replied, "If I cannot conquer him, I will consider myself a failure."

The rishi then told him, "This great enemy of whom I am speaking is the mind."

From that day on, the king tried everything to overcome the mind. He tried all kinds of techniques to gain control over his own mind.

Years passed and still he could not conquer the mind. Finally, the king had to admit that he had failed and that the mind is truly the strongest enemy.

The mind is powerful and will try every means possible to gain control over our soul. Many yogis and rishis have tried to gain control over their minds but failed. If such is the fate of those who have given up the world to conquer their own mind, then what is the fate of the rest of us who are immersed in the world?

The mind is the obstacle our soul must deal with to return to God. The mind is like a soccer goalie, guarding the goal. It will try everything to keep the ball from reaching the goal. If even devoted rishis had trouble overcoming the mind, how can we do it?

The fact is that we cannot conquer the mind on our own. The only way to conquer the mind and still it is through the help of someone who has conquered the mind. Such enlightened beings give us a lift to contact the Light and Sound within us. The Light and Sound help uplift our soul beyond the realm of mind.

The rishi found that doing spiritual practices alone in the jungle did not help him overcome the mind. The mind still tempted him with the countless desires of the world.

The mind knows that contact with the soul will render it harmless. Thus, the mind will find all kinds of excuses to keep us from meditation. It will make us think of the past. It will make us think of the future. It will make us wiggle around instead of sitting still. It will make us feel sleepy just when we sit to meditate. It will make us feel hungry. It will make us feel jealous. It will make us feel depressed. It will make us feel like doing work instead of meditating. It will find a million excuses.

How do we overcome the mind's tendencies to distract us? We must use the tendency of the mind to form positive habits. The mind likes habits. If we tell our mind that we need to sit for meditation each day at the same time and place, a habit will form. Soon we will find ourselves compelled to sit for meditation at that time each day. If we miss meditation, we will start to feel like something is amiss. Soon we will find ourselves meditating regularly.

When we learn to concentrate fully, wholly, and solely into the Light and Sound, we will experience bliss, peace, and joy. We will want to repeat meditation again and again because of the wonderful experience we receive.

Detachment

Nonattachment

One day a rich man came to Lord Buddha and said, "I see that you are the Awakened One. I am coming to you for some advice."

The Buddha asked him to share what was on his mind.

The rich man continued, "My life is focused on my work. Although I have made a lot of money, I am preoccupied with worry. Many people work for me and I am responsible for them. They depend on me for their success. Yet, I enjoy my work and enjoy working hard. When I met your followers they spoke of the importance of living the life of a recluse.

I also notice that you yourself were the son of a king, living in wealth and splendor, but you gave it up to wander as a homeless recluse looking for enlightenment. I want to know if I should do the same thing and give up my wealth. I want to do the right thing and be a blessing to my people. Should I also give up everything I have to find truth?"

The compassionate Buddha told him, "Anyone can receive the bliss of finding truth as long as he or she follows the path of unselfishness. If you are going to cling to your wealth, then it is better to throw it away than let it poison your heart. But if you do not cling to it, but use it wisely, then you will be a blessing to people. It is not wealth and power that make people slaves, but it is clinging to wealth and power that makes people enslaved."

Lord Buddha explained to him that his teaching did not require anyone to become homeless or give up the world unless he wants to. He explained it did require people to free themselves from the illusion that the body and world are their permanent and true home. He explained that his teaching required people to lead an ethical life.

"But," Lord Buddha explained, "whatever people do, either in the world or as a recluse, they should put their whole heart into it. People should be committed to whatever they do but full of energy. If they face struggles, they should do so without hatred or envy. People should live a life not of ego, but of truth, and then bliss will fill their soul."

These words spoken thousands of years ago are as true today as they were then. Nonattachment does not mean we have to give up our homes, our wealth, our families, and what we have received in life. It only requires that we give up attachment to these things. Whatever situation in which we find ourselves in life has come to us due to our karma. Some are born rich and others are born poor. Some gain money in life and others lose money in life. What is important is that we are not attached to our outer situation. If we are poor we should not curse God, and if we are rich we should not gloat. Our outer circumstance is a cup that has been handed to us. Within that circumstance, we can take care of our responsibilities to our family and community. For that we may have to work hard. But we should not be attached. Our attachment should be with God. Our attention should be on making sure our soul attains communion with God. That can be attained whether we are rich or poor.

Those who are blessed with wealth should make the best use of it by taking care of their family responsibilities and then sharing with others. We need not give up everything. We can live in the world and do the best we can, but keep our focus and attention on finding God. Our hearts can develop purity and an attitude of selfless service and sharing with others.

We need not be attached to our outer situation. We can work to make a living while also working to develop spiritually. If we are blessed with wealth, we need not throw it away, but we should use it to help others, and to benefit from having more free time to meditate and do selfless service.

The key is to live in the world, but not be attached to it.

Karma

Karma vs. Free Will

Around 300 years B.C., there was a Greek philosopher named Zeno who lived in Athens. One day, the philosopher caught his slave stealing. He decided to teach him a lesson by giving him a beating for stealing.

The slave, who was a bit of a philosopher himself, said, "Zeno, why are you beating me? It was fated that I should steal."

The philosopher Zeno quickly responded, "And it was fated that I should beat you for stealing!"

This story is rich in meaning for those who think about the question of karma. Many times people say that they committed a wrong because of their karma. They tend to confuse the law of karma with free will. The saints speak of human beings as having twenty-five percent free will. The other seventy-five percent of what happens to us in life is due to the reactions of our past karmas.

The karmic events in our life are those that are reactions of the past. They tend to be reactions that happen to us. Despite our best care to be safe, an accident befalls us without any explanation or reason. We may be working hard to make a living, and out of the blue we suffer a financial setback. We may live our lives as good people, but something bad happens to us. The law of karma is based on the belief that these seemingly unexplained events that occur in our lives are due to reactions from the past, either earlier in this life or in a previous life.

We may not have been trying hard to have something happen, but we have a stroke of seeming good luck and win a prize, get money out of the blue, or meet a special person with whom we fall in love and marry. We may suddenly meet good fortune out of the blue. All these events, both good and bad, that come to us without trying are usually the result of our past karma.

Some people use karma as an excuse to do wrong, but when it comes to our making a choice as to how to act in a certain situation, that usually falls under free will. It is not ordained that we break the law, hurt someone, or steal. Those are choices that we make in our own lives. We cannot blame God and our karmas for our shortcomings. We may come into life with our personality, but what we do is up to our choice or free will.

Just as Zeno and his slave used fate as the excuse for committing a wrong, when we do so ourselves, we are bound to get the reaction. The initial wrong might be due to free will, but the consequence then is our karmic debt that we incur.

As we live our life, we can live by the principle of "Be Good," as Sant Kirpal Singh Ji Maharaj said. We have free will to choose between committing good or evil. We need to take responsibility for our actions. Whatever we choose, we reap the reward or the punishment.

Rather than spend time pondering over what is our karma and what is free will, we should take it that we have choices to make and should always choose to do good over evil.

Spiritual Life

Choose Between the Dark or the Golden Age

In ancient India, one of the rulers was Yudhishthira. He lived in a time when spiritual values prevailed and people were filled with virtues. It was a period when spirituality was considered to be more important than material wealth.

In the last ten years of Yudhishthira's rule he started noticing a change in the people. People began answering the call of their lower self and they stopped listening to their conscience. He knew that the Kali Yuga, or the Dark Age, was on the horizon.

As Yudhishthira was sitting in his kingdom, two men came to have an audience with him. They had a grievance they wanted to settle, so they came to him for advice.

One man said, "I have bought a plot of land from this man, and after he sold it to me, I discovered there was a treasure buried there. Since I had only purchased the land from him, I want to return the treasure to him because I did not buy it from him and he is the rightful owner."

Yudhishthira was pleased at the honesty of the man who bought the land since he told the other man about the found treasure and even wanted to return it.

The man who sold the land said, "It is true that the treasure was mine, but when I sold him the land, he became the owner of the land and whatever is in it. Therefore, I would like him to keep the treasure."

The man who bought the land said, "Please take your treasure back. I do not want to carry the sin on my head of taking what is not rightfully mine."

The seller said, "Look, I have sold you the land along with whatever is in it. I cannot accept the treasure that now belongs to you. Please do not tempt me and lead me into greed."

Yudhishthira was highly pleased with the noble behavior of both these men.

The men said, "We cannot agree on what to do since we both want to give the treasure to the other. We have been arguing over this for days and we would like you to settle the case."

Yudhishthira thought over the situation and said to himself, "These two people are behaving nobly and ethically. I can see that the Kali Yuga, or the Dark Age, has not yet come. Let me wait and see what happens."

Yudhishthira said to them, "I want you both to come back to me in a week with this case." So the men left.

A week later, they both returned. Something had drastically changed. This time the case they presented to the king was different. Now they were both arguing to keep the treasure themselves.

The seller said, "I decided the treasure belonged to me. I sold him the land, but not the treasure."

The buyer said, "That is not right. Since I bought the land, everything in the land belongs to me!"

Yudhishthira saw that greed had now taken over their ethical sense. Yudhishthira realized that this was a sign that the Kali Yuga, or Dark Age, had come.

Yudhishthira ultimately settled the case by arranging the marriage of the son of one of them to the daughter of the other to keep the treasure in the family. But he knew that the age of spirituality and ethical living had come to an end.

Whether we are living in one age or the other, each human being has the choice to select how he or she wishes to live. It is a choice each can make in everyday life. Every day we have a choice whether to succumb to the greed and temptations of the Dark Age, or choose to live according to the spiritual values of the Golden Age. Living a spiritual life means putting in time for meditation so that we can reunite our soul with God. It means behaving in an ethical manner. It means choosing good over bad, nonviolence over violence, love over hatred, selfless service over greed, and truth over falsehood.

Being with Like-minded People

The company we keep is important for our spiritual growth. It is said, "A person is known by the company he or she keeps." If we spend time with rich people, we will think about money all the time. If we spend time with drunkards, we will be enticed to drink. If we hang around with gamblers, we will be easily influenced to gamble. If we stay around people who fight, we will tend to be argumentative ourselves.

The following account from the life of the great Chinese scholar, Mencius, illustrates this point.

Mencius's mother was a wise woman, as mothers generally are. During her lifetime, she moved her residence on three occasions for the sake of her son, Mencius. At first they lived near a graveyard. One day, she discovered that her son was pretending to be a mourner. The lad would watch the mourners at the cemetery as they attended funerals. Since children are impressionable, he would frequently imitate the behavior of the mourners. The mother was alarmed, so she decided to move.

Next, she moved to an area with markets and bazaars. After a while she noticed her son, Mencius, had started to play the role of shopkeeper. He would spread out their possessions, pretending he owned a shop. He started arguing with other people just as he had seen shopkeepers arguing with customers and other shopkeepers. The mother was upset about the influence this company had on her son, so she decided to move again.

127

This time, the mother selected a house near a school. Soon, she found Mencius imitating the scholars, researching subjects and learning about them. She was happy that this was the right influence on her son. He grew up to be one of the noted Chinese scholars.

This story illustrates the wisdom and sacrifice of a mother for her child to give him or her the best. It also illustrates the power of the company we keep.

If we wish to be an artist, we should spend time with artists. If we wish to be a doctor, we should spend time with people involved in the medical profession. If we wish to develop positive virtues, we should stay around people who exhibit goodness. If we wish to be spiritual, we should spend time in the company of spiritually minded people.

Our lives are precious. We come here with a fixed number of breaths. Within that time, we need to fulfill the purpose of our life. We can develop spiritually and be of service to others. Spending time with people who drag us down and pull our attention away from these goals is a waste of our life's breaths.

We should take a decision as to what we want in life. Once having taken that decision, we should work toward that goal. Spending time with like-minded people who have the same goals can help hasten our footsteps toward fulfilling the purpose of our life.

Prayer and Meditation

The True Purpose of Prayer

If one were to spend a day with God and listen in on all the prayers that reached God's ear, one would find most of them falling into two categories. One group would be praying to God because they wanted something from God. The other group would be praying to God out of fear, asking God to save them from the reactions of their sins. The following anecdote from the life of the great Sufi mystic woman saint, Rabia Basri, brings a new perspective to the question of prayer.

Rabia observed many of the people going to places of worship to perform various rituals while praying. She found that they would recite certain words while doing certain acts. She remarked to her close friends, "I find most people pray to earn some kind of merit from God. They pray so that they will enter heaven and avoid hell."

Her friends said, "Then what is the true purpose of prayer?"

Rabia replied, "To me, prayer is the means to enter God's presence and have intimate communion with God." Thus, she never relied upon the mechanical repetition of prayers as a means to win God's pleasure. Her prayers were spontaneous cries of the heart, yearning for union with her Beloved.

Her prayers carried the true expressions of her soul. One of her prayers that came forth from her soul was, "O God, whatever share of gifts and attainments of this world that are due to me, please give those instead to Your enemies, those who would curse and slander God's Name. Whatever share of the gifts of the world to come in heaven that You give me, please give them instead to Your friends, or those who love God. As for me, O Lord, You are enough for me!"

Rabia had realized the truth expressed by saints of all religions. They did not pray to God for things of this world. They did not pray in order to gain merit to enter heaven. The greatest saints and mystics were lovers of God and prayed only for the divine vision and ultimate union with God.

It is like being in love in a worldly sense. When two people are in love, they are content with each other's company. When a holiday comes and each asks the other what he or she wants the other to buy, a typical answer is, "Nothing, you are enough for me." Love is more fulfilling and satisfying than any worldly gifts. Similarly, those who are in love with the Lord are fulfilled by basking in God's divine bliss. They become so lost in this warm love that they need not ask God for things of this world. They are not interested in praying to God for material wealth, for name or fame, or for position or power. Their focus is on having union with the Lord.

Saints and mystics also did not pray for protection from going to hell and securing a seat in heaven. They only cared about being united with God. Their attitude is, "If God resides in heaven, that is where I want to be. If God resides in hell, then that is where I would rather be if I could be with my Beloved Lord."

Rabia's vision was so high that if she was due to receive gifts of the world, she preferred that God give them instead to people of the world who slandered God. Why? She knew that by receiving good fortune from God, people who had turned their backs on the Lord would turn their face to God in gratitude. She had so much love for her fellow human beings that she wanted them to know her Beloved God. If giving them her share of worldly gifts would create in them love for God, she was willing to sacrifice for them.

She also prayed that any gifts in the world to come that were coming her way should go instead to those who praised God. She felt that most of those she had seen who were devout and praised God were doing so because they wanted the gifts from the world to come. Thus, she wanted them to have her share because she herself was not interested in those types of gifts. What was then left for Rabia? She only wanted God alone. God was enough for her.

If we were to spend a day with God, we would find that it is only a rare few who pray to God for only God. Suchlike prayers catch God's attention. God is the giver and most people want God's gifts. God is moved by the prayers of those who want God alone. That is the true purpose of prayer.

Praying and Working

There is a beautiful German proverb that says, "Pray as though no work would help, and work as if no prayer would help."

The first part of the saying says that we should pray as if no work would help. In this kind of prayer, we are focusing all our attention in God. All our being is immersed in the prayer. It is as if we become the prayer itself. When we pray with such intensity and single-mindedness, God cannot ignore us.

There is the story of the mother who was cooking food in the kitchen. Suddenly, her child in the other room let out a blood-curdling scream. The mother dropped what she was doing and ran to pick up the child and comfort him. A few days later, while the mother was cooking, the child in the other room began to whimper, but the mother ignored him. The child, realizing the mother was ignoring him, tried whimpering again, but the mother again ignored him.

The child sheepishly crept into the kitchen and said to his mother, "Mommy, how is it that the other day you came running when I cried, but today you did not come?"

The mother replied, "The other day I could hear the pain in your voice, but today I knew from the tone that you were just faking it for my attention."

Similarly, God knows when our prayers are sincere. God knows when we are truly crying for the Lord. God knows when we are in pain and we truly want help. But if we are merely half-hearted in our prayer, then

God might or might not respond. That is why it is said that when a seeker is truly yearning for God, God hears it and will help that seeker find a way back to God.

There is another saying, "God hears the sincere cry of an ant sooner than the trumpeting of an elephant." This saying is instructing us that if we have a deep prayer for something, we should pray with our whole heart, soul, and mind as if no work would help us achieve what we want, and our prayer will certainly bear fruit.

The second part of the saying is that we should work as if no prayer would help. This is addressed to another group of people who will not pray, but will put in all efforts to attain what they want. Many feel that all they gain is due to their own efforts. They do not remember God or call on God for help. They do not realize God's presence or that God is a power that can help us. True spirituality involves a combination of both attitudes. We should do our part to take our share of responsibility, and then use our time to help others. We should work as hard as we can to fulfill our duties as if no prayer would help. In this, we would be fulfilling our responsibilities to ourselves, our family, our communities, and our world. We would be of use and of service to others. Then, after putting in our best effort, if we found we still did not succeed, we could pray with all our heart, soul, and mind for help.

Spirituality is the path of positive mysticism. We come into this world with certain responsibilities. We may have to support our family, we may have a certain role or job that we have to fill in this lifetime, and we have a collective responsibility to our society. We cannot shirk those duties to sit up on a mountaintop meditating all day and hoping God will provide for us. We need to spend time in meditation while also doing our duties allotted to us in life. Thus, when God sees we have put in our best efforts, and then, after all else fails, we turn to the Lord, God will take notice. But if we merely sit back and relax and expect God to do everything for us, that will not happen.

The same is true of our meditations. We should not think that if we only meditate for a few minutes once every few months that God will reward us. Rather, we should put in the required time with accuracy and full devotion. We should meditate regularly, accurately, and with full concentration. In this way, we are working as if no prayer would help. Then, if we have done our part, and we still do not achieve what we wanted, we should pray to God with all our heart, soul, and mind for help. If our yearning is sincere, God will listen.

We should take a look at these two aspects of ourselves. Are we putting in full effort as if no prayer would help? And after doing so, are we praying to God as if no work would help? If we do these two things, we will find that our progress will move forward steadily and we will be blessed by God.

What Should We Ask from God?

If we were to listen to the multitude of prayers uttered by humanity to God each day, we would find them to be divided into several categories. Some people pray for material wealth, possessions, or objects of this world. Some pray for good health or the miraculous cure of a disease either for themselves or a loved one. Some who are in danger pray for the safety of their lives or the lives of those they love. Some pray for fame and glory. Others, fame, power, and position. Some pray for success. Some pray for a relationship to be healed. Some pray to have a husband, a wife, or a child. We may wonder if one prayer is better than another. We may wonder what God wants us to pray for.

The following story supplies some guidance in answering that question. It is said that once there was a king with several queens. Necessity demanded that he leave them for a while to travel abroad. So he asked each of his queens what she wished him to bring back to her from his travels. One queen asked him to bring her expensive jewelry. Another queen asked him to bring back rich clothing that was beautifully designed. One asked for cosmetics. Another queen asked for fine decorations for the house. Another queen asked for special delicacies that would be rich and tasty. Finally, the king asked the youngest of the queens what she wanted him to bring back for her. This queen happened to love the king the most. She said that she did not want him to bring back anything for her. The only thing she wanted was for him to return to her quickly. She told him that she would be pining and longing in his absence, and that he should come back soon.

The king went abroad, and before returning, he made sure to find each of the things that his queens had requested. He picked up the expensive jewelry for one wife. He obtained the rich clothing for the other wife. He also purchased the cosmetics, the decorations, and the delicacies for the other three queens. When he reached his home, he had the gifts sent to each of the queens in their respective palaces. But he himself went directly to the palace of the queen who loved him the most and only wanted him. He was pleased that there was one queen who was not interested in riches and wealth, but only wanted him.

The queen thanked God for the grace given to her that her husband was with her and that she needed nothing else. Although the rest of the queens received what they wanted, none of them had the good fortune to receive the attention of her husband. All the riches they had were useless without love.

This story describes our condition in relationship to God. Most people are asking God for things of the world that are perishable. They all want gifts of one sort or the other. It is only the true lovers of God who want nothing from God but God. They do not care for riches or wealth. They do not care for name and fame. They do not care for anything of this world. All they want is God.

When we receive the gifts of this world, we still feel unsatisfied. We still feel as though there is something we are missing. The gifts of the world are of no help unless we have God. Once we have God, then we need nothing else to make us happy.

If we wish to pray to God for that which God wants the most to give us, we should pray to God for God. That prayer is the greatest.

Tolerance and Forgiveness

Tolerating Others

There is a story of a holy man from the Middle East who was in the habit of not eating breakfast each morning until a hungry person came by to share it with him. He felt that he should share his food with those in need. One day, an elderly man came by. The holy man saw him and invited him to share his breakfast with him.

The elderly man thanked him profusely. Then he sat down at the table to join him. As they began to say a blessing over the food, the elderly man said aloud a prayer to the pagan gods. This horrified the holy man who only believed in one God. He felt that the elderly man was a nonbeliever in God and became very upset. He jumped up and ordered the old man to leave his table.

"If you believe in pagans, then I don't want you in my house!" he said to the old man, who scurried off.

When the holy man returned to his table, he heard God speak to him. God said, "What right have you to send that man away?"

The holy man said, "He did not believe in You."

God replied, "Look here! I know he does not believe in Me. But I have been supplying the unbeliever with food every day for eighty years even though he doesn't believe in Me. Couldn't you tolerate him for one single meal?"

This anecdote conveys a powerful message. We sometimes become righteous about our own beliefs and our own goodness and look down upon others. Sometimes we do not understand or tolerate others with their faults. But if we think about this story, we realize that no matter how bad someone is, God provides him or her with everything needed to live and puts up with a wide range of people. There are people who lie, who cheat, who deceive others, and who slander others. There are people who hurt others and even kill others. There are people who steal and people who are selfish. So many people with numerous faults live upon this earth. There are people who believe in God and there are people who are atheists or agnostics. Yet, God provides life to each of them. God provides food and water to each of them. God provides air and sunlight to each of them. If God can provide for all kinds of people with all their faults, then surely each of us could do the same.

Even on the spiritual path, many feel righteous about ourselves. Some people criticize others who do not meditate as much as they do, who do not do as much service as they do, or who do not live by the ethical values as well as they do. Sometimes people become very outspoken about the faults of others. But have we ever analyzed our own selves? Is it our duty to become the reformers of others? We should instead be tolerant of others' faults. God knows everyone's faults. God sees everything we do and everything everyone else does. If God has to put up with the faults of others, then why can't we do the same?

The message of this story is that we should be kind and loving to all. We should respect and tolerate people who have different beliefs and customs from those we have. We should tolerate even those whom we feel do not believe in God or who do not believe in God in the same way we believe. God has made a world with people following many different religions and yet provides for each of them. Let us take a lesson and make sure we exercise tolerance toward others as we walk the highways of this world.

If we can have tolerance for others, then we are acting like true children of the Lord. God is love, and when we show tolerance for others, we too are filled with love and earn God's pleasure.

Enlightened Living

Enlightened Living

There is a quotation by the great Greek philosopher, Socrates. Once he said, "Our prayers should be for blessings in general, for God knows best what is good for us." This quote coincides with the prayer to God to give us whatever is good for us.

Time and again, whenever we demand something from God that is continually denied to us, it is usually because we are asking for something that is not for our ultimate good. There are many occasions when we persist in trying for something and do not give up. Sometimes we are given a lesson in that it is granted to us anyway, and we come to see that it was not in our best interest. Sometimes we go after something only to wish we had just sat back and let God give us what was best for us.

There have been many instances in which people prayed to God for something, and God did not grant their wish. Later they came to learn that receiving the wish would not have been a good thing after all. Will a mother allow the child to have poison? The child may cry for it and throw a tantrum, but if it is poison, the mother will not grant it. Instead the mother will give the child what is best for him or her. The child may not realize it at the time, but as the child grows and learns, the child is grateful for all the things the mother denied him or her that were ultimately not good.

Many people are anxious about making choices. We see games in which someone has to pick what is in the left hand or the right hand, or behind door number one or door number two. There is a lot of anxiety about making the wrong choice. How can we make the right choice? The way to be sure we make the right choices about what to pray for is to pray that God gives us what is best for us. God makes no mistake.

Rather than pray for something that may or may not be the best for us, let us pray for God's will for us. How many times have we found that when we left our fate in the hands of God, things worked out for the best? How many times does this have to happen for us to have faith and trust in the process?

God wants us to come Home. God wants us to live in eternal peace and bliss in the spiritual realm. When we make the decision to go back to God, then God opens all the doors for us. Then, if we pray to God to give us what is best for us, God will give us the fastest route back to our eternal Home. It is only we who delay our Homecoming by praying for things that take us in the opposite or different directions.

What are the spiritual pearls to enlightened living? If we relax and rest in God's will, we will find that everything works out for the best in the long run. Meditation is a process of relaxing in God's will. Meditation provides a time when we can let go of all clutching and praying for this thing and that. It is a time in which we sit in a state of stillness and surrender to God's will. It is a chance to let go of all our wants and desires. We merely sit in a receptive mood and ask God to grant what is best for us. We will find that God will give us more than we could ever imagine. That is the secret to enlightened living.

Through meditation, we will find the treasure of spiritual pearls to enlightened living that will bring us peace, happiness, and bliss.

About the Author

Sant Rajinder Singh Ji Maharaj is one of the world's leading experts in meditation. He has presented his powerful yet simple technique to millions of people throughout the world through seminars, meditation retreats, television and radio shows, magazines, and books. His method of achieving inner and outer peace through meditation has been recognized and highly respected by civic, religious, and spiritual leaders wherever he goes.

He is the author of many books and publications, including *Empowering Your Soul through Meditation*, *Inner and Outer Peace through Meditation*, with a foreword by H. H. the Dalai Lama, *Spiritual Thirst*, *Silken Thread of the Divine*, *Echoes of the Divine*, *Visions of Spiritual Unity and Peace*, *Ecology of the Soul and Positive Mysticism*, *Education for a Peaceful World*, and in Hindi, *Spirituality in Modern Times*, *Self Realization*, *Search for Peace within the Soul*, *Salvation through Naam*, *Spiritual Treasures*, *Experience of the Soul*, *Spiritual Talks*, and *True Happiness*, audiotapes, videotapes, and hundreds of articles which have been published in magazines, newspapers, and journals throughout the world. His programs are broadcast throughout the world on television, radio, and over the Internet.

For information, or to contact the author,
go to www.radiancepublishers.com,
or send an e-mail to: info@radiancepublishers.com